Methadone Maintenance Treatment
A Community Planning Guide

Mark Erdelyan
Colleen Young

camh

Centre for Addiction and Mental Health
Centre de toxicomanie et de santé mentale

Library and Archives Canada Cataloguing in Publication

Methadone Maintenance Treatment: A Community Planning Guide /
Mark Erdelyan & Colleen Young
ISBN: 978-0-88868-820-0 (PRINT)
ISBN: 978-0-88868-821-7 (PDF)
ISBN: 978-0-88868-822-4 (HTML)

PZ168

Printed in Canada

A reproducible copy of this publication is available on the Internet at www.camh.net.

For information about this or other Centre for Addiction and Mental Health resource
materials, or to place an order, please contact:

Publication Services
Tel.: 1 800 661-1111 or 416 595-6059 in Toronto
E-mail: publications@camh.net

Website: www.camh.net

Credits:
Development and writing: Mark Erdelyan, CAMH; Colleen Young, CY Health Communications
Editorial: Rachelle Redford, Write On!
Graphic design: Nancy Leung, CAMH
Print production: Chris Harris, CAMH
Typesetting: TC Communications Express

3707/ 03-2009 / PZ168

"From the time before the MMT program opened to today, it is the voices of our champions that are being listened to. The difference today is we now hear happy voices, see healthier individuals and families and interact with people who no longer merely exist but enjoy life again."

—MMT *program director*

Contents

Acknowledgements

This document was developed on behalf of the Centre for Addiction and Mental Health (CAMH) by Mark Erdelyan, Program Consultant, CAMH Windsor and Colleen Young, independent writer and instructional designer.

The development team would like to acknowledge the review committee for their support and feedback.

Reviewers
· Christie Collins-Williams (CAMH, Toronto)
· Al Cudmore (CAMH, Hamilton)
· Elizabeth Larocque (Algoma Public Health Methadone Program, Sault Ste. Marie)
· Janine Luce (CAMH, Toronto)
· Jean-Francois Martinbault (Sandy Hill Community Health Centre, Ottawa)
· Norma Medulun (Niagara Health System, St. Catharines)
· Lyle Nicol (CAMH, Thunder Bay)
· Karen O'Gorman (CAMH, Thunder Bay)
· Lynda Ruddock-Rousseau (Drouillard Road Clinic, Windsor)
· Peter Williams (CAMH, Ottawa)
· John Zarebski (CAMH, Chatham)

The guide was also reviewed by the Methadone Maintenance Treatment Provincial Initiatives Steering Committee.

We would like to offer a special thanks to Christine Bois (CAMH, OpiATE Project Manager) for her support throughout all phases of this project and to Sheila Lacroix (CAMH, Toronto) for her extensive literature search in preparation for the writing of this resource.

The 2009 edition is a revision of the 2000 edition of *Methadone Maintenance Treatment: A Community Planning Guide*. Funding for the guide was provided by the Government of Ontario.

Introduction

Methadone maintenance treatment (MMT) is recognized, in Canada and internationally, as an effective, safe and cost-effective treatment option for opioid[1] dependence. Although other forms of treatment continue to be explored, MMT remains the most widely used form of treatment for people who are dependent on opioids (Health Canada, 2002a). MMT can decrease the high cost of opioid dependence to individuals, their families and society (World Health Organization, 2004). Despite the research supporting MMT, public scepticism and myths about this form of treatment persist (Bell & Zador, 2000).

In its 2007 report, the Methadone Maintenance Treatment Practices Task Force recommended that the Ontario government improve access to MMT. The task force identified public resistance as a barrier to sustained access to MMT services, and recommended greater awareness of MMT and more intensive engagement of communities in the development of MMT services.

CAMH's Opiate Awareness, Treatment and Education (OpiATE) project is supported by funding from the Ontario Ministry of Health and Long-Term Care and is in partnership with the College of Physicians and Surgeons of Ontario (CPSO), Registered Nurses' Association of Ontario (RNAO) and the

---

1. opiate (n., adj.) naturally occurring substances—including morphine and codeine—found in opium (an extract from the seed pods of the opium poppy, Papaver somniferum L.). The term also refers to semi-synthetic opiate derivatives such as heroin and oxycodone. The term opiates is often incorrectly used to refer to all drugs with opium/morphine-like qualities, which are more properly classified under the broader term opioids.

opioid (n., adj.) any agent that binds to opioid receptors found in the brain and central nervous system. The four classes of opioids include: those naturally produced in the body (e.g., endorphins); opiates derived from opium (e.g., morphine, codeine); semi-synthetic opioids such as heroin and oxycodone; and fully synthetic opioids such as methadone that have structures unrelated to the natural opiates.

Reprinted with permission from the *User Guide for working with the documentary Prescription for Addiction* (2008).

Ontario Pharmacists' Association (OPA). The OpiATE project addresses the issues of opioid dependence in a way that builds on the work of the Methadone Maintenance Treatment Practices Task Force's report. CAMH believes that increased awareness and community engagement, along with professional supports, are critical in the development of an effective provincial response to the task force's recommendation. It is this commitment that led to the revision of this guide.

About this guide

This community planning guide is intended for those communities interested in starting or expanding MMT services. Community involvement is an important part of the planning, development and integration of an MMT program. The information in the guide is based on current research and first-hand experience. You will find practical suggestions on how to build public support and increase acceptance of those struggling with opioid dependence, through raising community awareness and acceptance of MMT services in your community. These suggestions are based on the experiences of four communities that were planning new or expanded services at the time of publication—Chatham-Kent, Halton, Ottawa and Thunder Bay.

The manual guides you through the stages of establishing a community working group, engaging the community, and planning, implementing and evaluating your program with the community. It is not a prescriptive step-by-step formula. Each community is different. You may wish to adapt some of the information to your situation. Moreover, your community working group may find that a re-ordering of the stages is more appropriate.

This guide complements other resource materials:
· *Methadone Saves Lives* http://methadonesaveslives.ca
· *Methadone Maintenance Guidelines* (CPSO) 2005
· *Methadone Maintenance Treatment: Client Handbook* (CAMH) 2008
· *Methadone Maintenance: A Physician's Guide to Treatment,* 2nd Edition (CAMH) 2008
· *Methadone Maintenance: A Pharmacist's Guide to Treatment,* 2nd Edition (CAMH) 2004

- *Methadone Maintenance: A Counsellor's Guide to Treatment* (CAMH) 2003
- *Methadone Maintenance Treatment: Best Practices in Case Management* (CAMH) 2009 (in press)
- *Best Practices Methadone Maintenance Treatment* (Health Canada) 2002
- *Report of the Methadone Maintenance Treatment Practices Task Force* (Government of Ontario) 2007.

For a listing of resources, see *Resources* on page 93.

About methadone maintenance treatment

Methadone maintenance is a medical treatment that can help people manage their addiction to opioids. This treatment can help people who are dependent on opioids get the medical and social support they need to stabilize and improve their lives.

What is opioid dependence?

Opioids are a family of drugs used to relieve pain. Some opioids, such as morphine and codeine, are made from the opium poppy plant. Other opioids are synthetically made from chemicals. Heroin is a highly addictive, illegal opioid made by adding a chemical to morphine.

Commonly misused prescription drugs include:
· oxycodone (e.g., Percodan, Percocet, OxyContin)
· hydrocodone (e.g., Tussionex)
· codeine (e.g., Tylenol 1, Tylenol 3)
· morphine
· hydromorphone (e.g., Dilaudid)
· meperidine (e.g., Demerol)

Opioids are effective painkillers. They can also create feelings of intense pleasure or euphoria. People who misuse or abuse opioids can easily become addicted to them.

QUICK FACT ▶

According to CAMH's 2007 *Ontario Student Drug Use and Health Survey*, 21% of students (grades 7–12) surveyed reported using prescription opioid pain relievers for non-medical purposes and almost 72% reported obtaining the drugs from home.

Opioid dependence develops after using opioids regularly for a period of time. Opioid dependence is not just a heavy use of opioids, but a complex health condition that includes both a psychological and physical dependence on opioids. People are psychologically dependent when a drug is so central to their thoughts, emotions and activities that the need to keep using the drug becomes a craving or compulsion. With physical dependence, the body has adapted to the drug and will suffer withdrawal symptoms if use of the drug is reduced or stopped abruptly.

Many people believe that dependence on opioid drugs is self-inflicted and efforts to treat people who are dependent on opioids will inevitably fail. Not so. Opioid dependence is a brain-related medical disorder for which there are effective treatments. No single treatment is effective for all individuals with opioid dependence. Two main treatment options are available:
· addiction treatment counselling (e.g., withdrawal management, out-patient, day treatment, residential or self-help/support group settings)
· substitution drug therapies using methadone or buprenorphine[2].

Treatment with methadone is safe and effective for many people who are dependent on opioids, especially when combined with counselling. To date, MMT remains the most widely used form of treatment for opioid addiction in Canada (Health Canada, 2002a).

About prescription opioids

Methadone isn't used just to treat people who are dependent on heroin. In fact, more and more people in Canada turn to methadone after struggling with prescription painkiller dependence. Prescription painkillers have become the predominant form of opioid use in many parts of

---

2. Buprenorphine is an alternative treatment to methadone. Two formulations of buprenorphine hydrochloride—Subutex and Suboxone—have recently been approved by Health Canada for use in treating opioid dependence. Subutex contains only buprenorphine hydrochloride. Suboxone tablets contain buprenorphine hydrochloride and naloxone, which deters abuse of the product by causing withdrawal symptoms if the product is injected rather than taken orally as prescribed (Collège des médecins du Québec and Ordre des pharmaciens du Québec, 2008; CPSO, 2009a).

Canada. Many opioid users report that they first used prescription opioids to treat pain. Research shows that a substantial proportion of prescription opioids are obtained directly or indirectly (e.g., through friends or partners) from sources in the medical system (Brands et al., 2004; Fischer et al., 2006).

In 2005–06, 46.5% of the people in MMT programs in Ontario were coping with dependence related to over-the-counter codeine preparations or prescription opioids compared to 15.7% who had heroin or opium problems (Hart, 2007).

◀ QUICK FACT

HOW DOES SOMEONE BECOME OPIOID DEPENDENT?

Opioid drugs are very effective painkillers. The strength of an opioid drug and the dose can be adjusted to address the intensity of pain, as needed. For example, if you break your arm, you might be moaning and groaning when you get to the hospital. But once your doctor gives you an injection of morphine, you can be reasonably comfortable while the doctor sets your arm and puts it in a cast. Before you go home, you are given a prescription for codeine pills so you won't have to suffer while the arm gets better.

For most people, a situation like this would be the only time they would take opioid drugs. Once the pain of the injury becomes tolerable, people usually stop taking prescription painkillers and don't give them a second thought.

But what if the pain doesn't go away? What if the only thing that can bring relief is opioid drugs? Then, you might continue to take them, and since you like the way they make you feel, you get some more. After a while, if they're not working as well as they used to, you might take more at a time or try a stronger opioid. You may think you could stop whenever you want to. But when you try to stop, you get very sick and can't stop thinking about starting up again. Eventually much of your time, energy and interest may be absorbed in getting and taking drugs. Your body has adapted to having the drugs and now you feel like you have to have them.

Continued on page 8

How does someone become opioid dependent?...Continued from page 7

Of course, this is only one example of how opioid dependence can begin. Some people start taking opioids for fun, seeking out a new experience and finding one that is pleasurable and predictable for a while. Some people may be looking for relief from poverty, emotional hardship or depression. Some may be drawn to the reckless image of the drugs, wanting to see themselves as "cool" or "hip."

Once a person starts taking opioids, they may continue using them for a long time, even though they know opioids are dangerous and that the pleasures are short-lived and superficial. They know the drugs keep them away from people and things that matter to them. Their health, home, finances and relationships may slip into a state of chaos. They need a chance to put the struggle with the drugs aside and take time and effort to sort out the rest of their lives. This is when treatment, such as methadone maintenance treatment, can help.

Adapted with permission from *Methadone Maintenance Treatment: Client Handbook* (CAMH) 2008.

What is MMT?

People who are dependent on opioids can take methadone to help stabilize their lives and reduce the harm related to their drug use.

Methadone maintenance treatment (MMT) is a substitution therapy. Substitution therapy replaces the drug that the person is dependent on with a prescribed substance that is pharmacologically similar, but safer when taken as prescribed. Substitution therapy can be used to manage nicotine as well as opioid dependence. Since its introduction in the 1960s, MMT continues to be an effective and widely used form of treatment for people who are dependent on opioids (Health Canada, 2002b).

Methadone is a long-acting opioid drug. This means it acts more slowly in the body and for a longer period of time than most other opioids. By acting slowly, it can prevent withdrawal symptoms and reduce or eliminate drug cravings, without causing a person to "get high". Because people enrolled in an MMT program have access to a reliable supply of legal, pharmaceutical-grade medication, they no longer have to suffer the stresses of getting illicit opioids, which may involve criminal activities and high-risk sexual practices. MMT helps people who are dependent on opioid drugs stabilize their lives, increasing the time and opportunity to deal with their health, psychological, family, housing, employment, financial and legal issues.

Medically supervised methadone treatment works best when combined with other types of health and social support services. These services include addiction counselling, case management, mental health services, health promotion, disease prevention and education, and other community-based services, such as legal, financial, medical, child care, dental and housing services (Health Canada, 2002a; NIH Consensus Conference, 1998).

MMT is a long-term treatment, lasting from one to two years to 20 years or more (World Health Organization, 2004; Centre for Addiction and Mental Health, 2008). The length of treatment depends on the person. Prolonged treatment with proper doses of methadone is medically safe and effective.

> **Short-acting opioids, such as heroin, must be taken frequently (three to four times a day) to avoid withdrawal. Methadone is most often administered once a day under medical supervision. (Split doses may be used in some situations, e.g., for women who are pregnant.) Treatment should include other support services, such as counselling (College of Physicians and Surgeons of Ontario, 2005).**

◀ QUICK FACT

What are the benefits of MMT?

Opioid dependence is a costly social problem. An estimated 30,000 people between the ages of 15 and 49 in Ontario regularly used illegal opioids in 2003 (Hart, 2007). If left untreated, opioid dependence creates significant costs related to medical care, drug treatment, lost productivity, criminal activity and an increase in the transmission of human immunodeficiency virus (HIV), hepatitis C virus (HCV) and other blood-borne diseases.

Methadone is the most effective treatment currently available for opioid dependence. It has been rigorously studied and has yielded the best results. MMT benefits not only the people receiving treatment (clients), but also their families, their communities and society as a whole.

Evidence from numerous controlled trials, large studies and program evaluations (World Health Organization, 2004; Health Canada, 2002b) has consistently shown that MMT can significantly reduce
· illegal use of opioids
· criminal activity
· deaths due to overdose
· behaviours that increase the risk of HIV transmission
· public health risks.

MMT improves
· physical and mental health
· social functioning
· quality of life
· pregnancy outcomes.

MMT can be provided in a community-based setting where treatment is administered on an outpatient basis. The longer clients stay in treatment, the more likely they are to reduce their illicit use of opioids and remain crime-free. Receiving treatment in a community that offers support through additional integrated components, such as counselling and health and social support services, gives clients more time and opportunity to deal with other important issues while they are in treatment. For example, they can receive care and guidance about major health and mental health concerns, as well as family, housing, employment, financial and legal issues. This, in turn, increases the likelihood that clients will stay in treatment (Hart, 2007; Health Canada, 2002c).

BENEFITS TO CLIENTS AND THE COMMUNITY

	BENEFITS TO MMT-TREATED CLIENTS	BENEFITS TO THE COMMUNITY
MMT reduces crime	• spend less time dealing drugs • spend less time involved in criminal activities	• less violence • fewer drug offence arrests • less crime (people with addictions no longer need to finance their addiction) • less prostitution • reduced criminal justice system costs
MMT improves health	• can stabilize their mood and functional state • can find improved access to health care • reduce their use of illegal opioids • reduce their use of other substances including cocaine, marijuana and alcohol • have a lower risk of death due to overdose • reduce injecting, and use of contaminated needles • reduce their risk of transmitting and contracting HIV and sexually transmitted infections • can receive education about harm reduction techniques from care providers • have better pregnancy and birth outcomes	• fewer discarded used needles • reduced spread of infectious disease • service providers educate drug users in harm reduction techniques, such as how to prevent HIV/AIDS, hepatitis and other health problems that might endanger the community • decreased public health risks • fewer pregnancy-related complications
MMT improves social functioning and promotes healthier community	• spend less time looking for and using narcotics daily • spend less time in jail • increase their likelihood of getting employment • can improve their family relations • can improve their parenting skills • can improve their overall social functioning and quality of life	• a safer and healthier neighbourhood • improved family functioning • lower unemployment rates • improved economic productivity • fewer homeless people • fewer people relying on social assistance

(Health Canada, 2002c; World Health Organization, 2004; Pang et al., 2007; Bell & Zador 2000; Health Canada, 2002a)

Cost benefits and cost effectiveness

There is clear evidence that the benefits of MMT far outweigh the costs of treatment (Health Canada, 2002b). MMT reduces the criminal behaviour associated with illegal drug use, promotes health and improves social productivity, all of which serve to reduce the societal costs of drug addiction.

Researchers in the U.S. found the annual costs of MMT to be considerably less expensive than the alternatives, such as no treatment, imprisonment or drug-free treatment programs. Criminal activities related to opioid use resulted in social costs that were four times higher than the cost of MMT. For every dollar spent on MMT, there is a savings to the community of between US$4 and $13 (Health Canada, 2002c).

In Canada, similar cost savings have been identified. The untreated opioid user can cost society an average $49,000 per year. However, it costs approximately $6,000 annually to treat a client with methadone, including the cost of medication, urine testing and physician care, nursing and counselling staff (Health Canada, 2002c).

COMPARING COSTS

MMT-TREATED CLIENTS	UNTREATED OPIOID DEPENDENCE
· Lower annual costs to society	· Higher annual costs to society
· $1 spent on MMT	· $4–13 in health and social costs
· $6,000 per person per year	· $49,000 per person per year

MMT costs less and people are more likely to stay in an MMT program compared to other types of treatment for opioid dependence, such as drug-free treatment, therapeutic communities and addiction treatment. One study found the cost effectiveness of MMT compared to other treatments was 4:1 (Health Canada, 2002c).

The *Joint WHO/UNODC/UNAIDS Statement on Substitution Maintenance Therapy* maintains that, by conservative estimates, every dollar invested in opioid dependence treatment programs may yield a cost savings of between $4 and $7 in reduced drug-related crime, criminal justice costs and theft. When health care-related savings are included, total savings can exceed costs by a ratio of 12:1 (World Health Organization, 2004).

◀ QUICK FACT

Providing comprehensive MMT to 15,000 people who are dependent on opioids costs an estimated $90 million a year. The personal and social cost to society for these individuals is seven times this amount: $660 million (Hart, 2007).

How is MMT delivered?

MMT is highly regulated and controlled, both federally and provincially. The Office of Controlled Substances, Health Canada, works with provincial and territorial governments and medical licensing bodies to help increase access to MMT (Health Canada, 2002a). Provincial and territorial governments and medical licensing bodies are responsible for the development of standards and guidelines for methadone treatment. Since methadone is a controlled drug, only those physicians who have received an exemption under the federal *Controlled Drugs and Substances Act, 1996* can prescribe methadone. (For more information about training and exemption, see *Recruit service providers* on page 58 and *Training for service providers* on page 72.)

In Ontario, the College of Physicians and Surgeons of Ontario (CPSO) administers the application and assessment processes of physicians and recommends to Health Canada the names of physicians for consideration of an exemption to prescribe methadone. The Ontario College of Pharmacists (OCP) is the registering and regulating body for pharmacy practice, including the dispensing of methadone. The 14 Local Health Integration Networks (LHINs) fund, plan and integrate health care services at the regional and local levels.

In the community, MMT services are delivered in a range of settings. The most common delivery models are the clinic model and the office-based practice model or a combination of these two called the tiered-care model. Whichever model a community adopts, there are many possible variations in how the services are delivered.

Clinic model: The clinic model (secondary-care setting) offers a comprehensive MMT program that includes both health and social supports in one location. The convenience of the one-stop clinic model saves time and expenses for the client and ensures that the clients' quality of life issues are addressed. It also facilitates better coordination and communication among the service providers. Communities that don't have the resources to support a single clinic site can look for ways to simulate this type of coordinated and integrated model by establishing referral protocols with other service providers and partners. It is important to find ways to refer clients to services that can effectively meet their needs.

Office-based practice model: The office-based practice model delivers a comprehensive MMT program in several locations. Primary-care doctors see methadone clients in their medical practice, either during their regular office hours or at specifically assigned time periods. While pharmacy and laboratory service are often available close to doctors' offices, clients may have to travel to other support services.

Tiered-care model: The tiered-care model combines the clinic and office-based practice models. New clients start their treatment in a clinic setting. Once their treatment reaches a stabilization, or maintenance, stage, their care can be transferred to a primary-care physician for ongoing MMT. If a client requires more intense care, the client can be transferred back to the clinic.

Treatment programs that focus on maintaining clients in treatment are the most likely to succeed. Offering comprehensive services that address the multiple and evolving needs of clients leads to higher treatment-retention rates. Office-based practice and tiered-care models should develop partnerships with community-based health and social support services to ensure clients receive the comprehensive services they need. Services should develop a clear referral protocol. (See *Policies and procedures* on page 73.) Whichever delivery model your community chooses, flexibility, innovation and collaboration play an important role in achieving positive treatment outcomes.

> *"Methadone does a great job of addressing the physical aspects of opioid dependence… but in terms of the psychological, social and spiritual aspects, in order for someone to get better from their addiction, you need to address those as well."*
> —*family physician and* MMT *prescriber*

People who are dependent on opioids are a diverse group of men and women of all ages, with varying socioeconomic circumstances, from different cultural backgrounds and involved in different types of relationships and family situations. They may live in urban, rural or remote areas. They may have other physical or mental health problems in addition to their dependence on opioids. They do not all have the same type or level of need for treatment. And as treatment progresses, a client's needs will likely change. It is important to recognize client diversity and their evolving needs.

Components of an MMT program

Because the needs of clients are so diverse, the delivery of MMT usually involves a large, multidisciplinary network of professionals from many different disciplines and backgrounds, including medicine, counselling, substance use treatment and rehabilitation, social work, mental health, community support, corrections and others. At the minimum, MMT delivery requires physicians, pharmacists and laboratory services. The roles and responsibilities of the different service providers may vary or overlap depending on a number of factors, such as program setting, available resources and geographic location.

Communities whose population is spread over a large geographic area may consider exploring the feasibility of telemedicine.   ◁   TIP

An integrated comprehensive program would include some or all of the following:
· methadone
· medical care
· other substance use treatment
· counselling and support
· mental health services
· health promotion, disease prevention and education
· links with community-based social support services
· outreach and advocacy.

POSSIBLE COMPONENTS OF AN MMT PROGRAM

SERVICE PROVIDER	RESPONSIBILITIES
Physicians	· patient assessment · methadone dosing · analysis and review of urine screen results · administration of take-home carries program · communication with other service providers, especially pharmacists · substance abuse counselling (if provided by physician) · pain management (if physician is acting as family physician) · general health care (if physician is acting as family physician and/or nurse practitioner) · screening, treatment and referral to family physician or specialists for infectious diseases (e.g., hepatitis B, hepatitis C, acute hepatitis, sexually transmitted infections, HIV, tuberculosis) · referral to related health and social support services
Pharmacists	· preparation and dispensing of methadone · education and counselling related to MMT · direct observation of dosing · assist in minimizing diversion and other problems · communication with physician
Laboratory services staff	· collection of urine samples · supervision of collection process or measures (e.g., temperature strips) to reduce tampering of specimens · analysis of urine samples · communication with physician and/or pharmacy Note: These services may be conducted by clinic staff on site.
Case managers and counsellors	· counselling · crisis counselling · case management, client support in accessing treatment services · ongoing assessment and adjustment of clients' treatment program · client care coordination and integration of services · referral to other health and social support services · client advocacy · client recruitment and outreach
Addiction treatment agency professionals	· assessment and treatment planning · case management · client recruitment and outreach · substance abuse counselling

Continued on page 17

Possible components of an MMT program...Continued from page 16

	· withdrawal management (if applicable) · supportive housing · referral to other health and social support services
Social services professionals	· assistance, support and referral to social services, such as: financial, housing, legal, transportation, child care, parenting, marriage and family counselling, working with child welfare agencies, education, employment, legal issues, home management
Primary health care professionals	· management of general health care concerns · pain management · counselling and health education · prevention, screening and treatment of infectious diseases
Nurses	· administration of methadone · observation of clients' general condition · counselling and health education · security of methadone · collection of blood samples · supervision of urine controls · client care coordination with other agencies on clients' behalf · training nursing staff and other disciplines
Mental health professionals	· assessment · treatment of psychiatric disorders · case management · referral to other health and social support services
Criminal justice and corrections personnel	· referral to MMT system · counselling support · provision of methadone for incarcerated clients
AIDS and HIV/IDU organization personnel	· health promotion and health education (e.g., safer sex) · counselling · group support · client recruitment and outreach · referral to other health and social support services
Needle exchange program staff	· needle exchange · health education · client recruitment and outreach · referral to other health and social support services

Sean's Story

My name is Sean. I'm 28 years old and I have been opioid dependant for 10 years. My life has done a complete 180 since I started MMT 5 years ago; I went from the brink of suicide to finding ways to live my life with new meaning. I now feel that I have something valuable to contribute to my community.

At age 17, I was prescribed Percocet after my wisdom teeth were removed. This opioid made me feel powerfully euphoric and relieved the depression and anxiety I felt as a teen. However, when I came down from it, I felt more depressed than ever and began seeking out any drug that would make me feel euphoric. A year later, I was re-introduced to opioids when my employer started paying me with prescription OxyContin when she was low on money. I didn't recognize the toll the drugs were taking. They gave me tremendous physical energy that allowed me to work 18-hour days, and they helped relieve my depression. But as my dependence increased, I needed more and more to get high. Eventually, getting and paying for opioids had become a full time job. I started growing and selling marijuana to pay for my $300-a-day opioid dependence.

As I became more desperate, I engaged in progressively riskier activities to support my habit. My life spiralled completely out of control. I tried to stop using, but the sickness and depression I felt in withdrawal made life without opioids seem worse than death. My life came to a crossroads when I realized that I had exhausted all my sources of income and that there was no way that I could continue. Lying on the floor of my apartment, I tried to decide if I had enough OxyContin left to kill myself or if I should just jump off the balcony. Then I remembered an ARF (Addiction Research Foundation) pamphlet I had tucked away and decided to call the number on the back to ask for help. They gave me the number to a methadone clinic and explained that if I could hang on for one more day they could help.

Continued on page 19

Sean's Story...Continued from page 18

Within a week of starting methadone treatment, I was able to completely stop my illicit opioid use and illegal methods of getting them.

Methadone helped to stabilize me and continues to provide a lifeline for me today. I was also fortunate to have found a terrific counsellor to talk to about my addiction. I have my health back. I'm working again and studying at university. My friends and family are a part of my life again, and they have been willing to learn and understand about addiction. I feel good about the advocacy and public education I am doing with a methadone maintenance planning group. I can't stress enough how important a role methadone played in stabilizing my life and helping me to make these positive changes. Methadone saved my life.

Getting
ready

Although the efficacy of MMT is well established, it is not without controversy. It is important to anticipate, identify and address attitudes and values opposed to MMT during the planning stages. Careful planning can help reduce problems that can delay or even stop the development of MMT services.

What to expect

You may meet opposition and challenges when proposing the development of MMT services in your community. It is not uncommon to hear such questions as "Why would you want to give drug users more drugs?" or "If we start a methadone program in our community, won't all the drug users move into this area?" or "Crime is going to increase. Our neighbourhood won't be safe anymore."

Most often, opposition stems from:
· process issues, for example how and when the community is consulted and whether the concerns of the community are being addressed
· prejudice and fears about people who are dependent on opioids, particularly fears about safety and exposure to people who are dependent on opioids
· lack of understanding or misperceptions about opioid dependence
· fear of depreciation of the neighbourhood, such as property values, traffic, noise and property management.

"The perception of the scary client who doesn't get better simply isn't true. I can see changes in people very quickly after they start on the program."

—family physician and MMT prescriber

Community opposition can be discouraging and time consuming. But you can have success if you:
· understand the level of the community's awareness and acceptance of MMT
· demonstrate the need for MMT in the community
· educate and engage the community.

If your community already has MMT services, residents may ask why their community needs more. Review your community's history of MMT and assess the general level of awareness and acceptance to this type of treatment.

Engaging the community on page 41 offers guidance on how you can engage the community to help your project succeed as well as how you can anticipate and resolve opposition.

Identify and verify your community's needs

You need to show both opponents and supporters that MMT services are needed in your community or that current services need expanding. Research the history of opioid addiction treatment and MMT in your community. Find facts and figures that clearly identify and confirm your community's need for MMT and that can help answer important questions, such as:
· How many people in your community are opioid users?
· How many of these opioid users are potential candidates for a methadone program?
· What client and community needs are not being met?
· How many community members are travelling outside the community to get MMT services?
· How many clients are on a waiting list to get into a local MMT program?

◁ TIP

Completing a thorough needs assessment is a large task. Researching and finalizing a comprehensive needs assessment report can be done by the community working group, a subcommittee of the group or a graduate student from a recognized university. Some communities form their working group before completing the needs assessment report. (See *Establishing a community working group* on page 27.)

It is unlikely that you will find statistics and survey results that will answer these questions directly. However, there are agencies and services in the community that can help you with your research and give you information that can support your project.

College of Physicians and Surgeons of Ontario

CSPO administers the provincial methadone program for physicians on behalf of the Ministry of Health and Long-Term Care. (For more information, see the CPSO listing in *Resources* on page 93.) CPSO can provide statistics about the number of people in your community who are receiving MMT, where MMT services are offered and how far people in your community are travelling to get treatment.

MMT is a province-wide initiative supported by a number of provincial groups including the Ministry of Health and Long-Term Care, College of Physicians and Surgeons of Ontario, Ontario College of Pharmacists, Ontario Pharmacists' Association, Registered Nurses' Association of Ontario and Centre for Addiction and Mental Health. Together, they strive to improve the quality and accessibility of MMT in Ontario.

◀ QUICK FACT

Needle exchange programs

Community needle exchange programs may be able give you useful data, such as the number of needles that have been exchanged since the program's inception, an estimate of the number of clients who are opioid users or how many have been asking about MMT. If there are no needle exchange programs in your area, consult programs nearby. Members of your community may be travelling to exchange their needles.

MMT clinics

Find out about existing MMT clinics and services available in your community or in nearby communities. Assess their operation, how they deliver services and their capacity. How are they accepted in the community? What can you learn from their experiences? Who are their partners?

MMT clients and potential clients

Conduct a needs assessment survey of clients and potential clients. You may also consider gathering information using a focus group. Survey and focus group results can give you valuable information that can demonstrate the community's need for MMT services, such as:
· the number of people who are dependent on opioids who are not getting MMT or another form of treatment
· the number of people receiving MMT
· where they have to go to get treatment
· what they like or dislike about MMT service delivery
· their reasons for not wanting to start or continue treatment
· the type of services they need.

Local agencies, such as addiction treatment agencies (including assessment and referral centres and withdrawal management services), needle exchange programs, health units and hospital emergency departments, may be able to help you recruit willing survey participants.

A client survey can also indicate whether clients are familiar with MMT and give you information to help shape your future awareness and education strategy. (See *Develop your awareness outreach strategy* on page 44.)

Other community agencies

Other community agencies that may be able to provide information to help you identify and verify the need for MMT include:
· addiction treatment providers
· LHIN
· public health units
· hospital emergency departments

- mental health agencies
- harm reduction programs
- AIDS organizations
- social services
- Ontario Works
- Children's Aid Societies
- supportive housing organizations
- police services
- corrections agencies.

According to data from CPSO, over 22,000 clients are receiving MMT across Ontario as of February 2009 (CPSO, 2009b). ◀ QUICK FACT

Listen and learn

As you collect information from community partners and agencies, listen to the people you interview. They are potential supporters and advocates.

These supporters can help you:
- understand the community's attitude towards MMT
- identify potential problematic issues
- learn more about the needs of the community
- tailor your program to the particular needs of your community
- find a key supporter and strong spokesperson to champion the cause
- gather anecdotal evidence to support your project.

You can call upon these supporters to:
- join your community working group
- be a supportive voice at community meetings
- speak on your project's behalf
- conduct information sessions among peers and to the public
- write letters of support.

Organize your findings

Organize your findings in a clear, concise report. As you prepare the best way to describe your project to both supporters and opponents, consider the following questions:

· Have you found ways of describing your initiative that seem to resonate with the people you have interviewed?
· When did you have to clarify or explain yourself?
· How are supporters describing the benefits of your initiative?
· What are opponents saying about you or about other MMT service providers?
· What are their main concerns?

Establishing a community working group

The community working group is made up of individuals interested in MMT, drug addiction and mental health, including representatives from local agencies and organizations. These supporters help "champion the cause" by promoting the program to the community, colleagues and media. The success of a MMT program depends on the hard work and ongoing support of the working group.

What does a community working group do?

The community working group:
· shares information about the community
· stays in touch with the attitudes (and changing attitudes) of the community
· confirms the need for MMT services in their community
· develops or finalizes a needs assessment report
· develops an action plan
· identifies potential barriers and possible solutions
· engages service providers in dialogue and participation
· educates the community about MMT
· oversees the implementation of the plan
· monitors the MMT program's success and needs.

The main goal of the working group is to prepare an action plan. This plan:
· confirms the need for MMT services in the community
· describes the strategy that will be used to achieve short- and long-term goals

· outlines the treatment delivery model (See *How is* MMT *delivered?* on page 13.)
· details the types of support services to be offered
· outlines how these services will be delivered
· delineates what resources partner agencies can contribute.

TIP ▷

Some working groups are formed before the needs assessment is done. In this case, the first goal is to establish consensus that there is a need for MMT services in the community. If it is agreed that there is a need, then the group moves ahead with the action plan.

The working group reviews the initiative and the needs assessment report, and identifies any oversights or new developments. Upon establishing consensus, the working group develops an action plan suited to the needs of the community.

Use the action plan to:
· secure funding from your local LHIN or other potential sources
· educate and engage the wider community
· monitor the project's progress
· celebrate achievements (milestones along the way).

A well-executed action plan founded on consensus among the working group members can lead to the successful establishment or expansion of MMT services.

Sometimes a working group may decide not to create an MMT program in their community. If this happens, the working group can still play an important community role. For example, it can meet to monitor trends in opioid drug use and determine whether MMT services may be needed in the future.

Build the community working group

While you are gathering information to determine the need for MMT services in your community, you will be compiling a list of supporters. These supporters should be among the people you invite to join the working group. Ask them to also recommend other people who could be invited to participate.

◁ TIP

Expect the unexpected. Sometimes, people you thought or assumed would be supportive of methadone treatment may, in fact, not be. Even people who provide addiction services may have misconceptions about MMT and may be resistant to developing such services in the community.

Do not hesitate to invite opponents as well as supporters. People or organizations who initially do not want MMT services in the community can provide insightful feedback. What the working group learns from opponents and the nature of their challenges will ensure a strong action plan. This information can also help prepare the awareness and education strategy. It is better to have opponents be part of the working group rather than operating against the project outside the group. People or organizations you thought might oppose your project could end up being your biggest supporters.

Meet with potential working group participants individually to discuss the initiative and to invite them to be a part of the working group.
· Explain the reasons for the project.
· Make clear what the benefits are for clients, the community and the potential partner.
· Outline the role of the working group.
· Describe what they can contribute to the working group and the project.
· Finish by inviting them to the initial meeting.

You may consider inviting:

Community partners
Community partners offer important insight into the community's needs, attitudes, values and resources. They can also share their subject-matter expertise, skills and experience, as well as knowledge specific to the community.

Community partners to consider include:
· addiction service providers
· LHIN staff
· representatives of community agencies, such as public health units, needle exchange programs, psychiatrists, mental health agencies, harm reduction programs, AIDS organizations, supportive housing organizations and social services departments

· MMT providers from nearby communities
· members of the local police department or correction services
· leaders of the community's Aboriginal or ethnocultural community, such as a First Nations Chief or Elder.

Community partners expect to be consulted and may be insulted if they are overlooked or deliberately ignored. Be inclusive when sending out invitations to join the working group.

Health care professionals and service providers

Invite health care professionals who already work with MMT clients as well as potential service providers, such as doctors, pharmacists, community nurses and staff from local laboratory services. They can provide feedback in the early planning stages that can help ensure successful implementation of MMT services tailored to their practice and the clients and community's needs.

Clients and family members

MMT clients and family members of clients are valuable additions to the working group. They can be an excellent source of information on the needs and perspectives of opioid users and methadone clients. Their first-hand experiences offer compelling stories to support your community education and media outreach efforts.

Be aware that some clients may feel uncomfortable participating in the working group. It may be intimidating for clients to be in a room with professionals, possibly including their own methadone doctor. You can offer them support by:
· including two or more clients in the group so they have peer support
· offering them a pre-meeting orientation session to give them an idea of what they can expect
· offering them a post-meeting session or counselling to help them deal with any sensitive issues that may have surfaced during the meeting
· paying them an honorarium for their participation and to help defer costs, such as travel or child care.

"Having a client involved in our community working group was key. These are the people who feel the stigma and can share their first-hand experiences to help develop a program that fits the community."

—*CAMH program consultant*

Professional consultant

The professional consultant offers support and guidance to the chairperson of the working group or may be chosen by the group to be the chair. The consultant may be someone from within the working group, a service provider or an outside facilitator. The professional consultant could be a CAMH staff member.

CAMH staff member

A CAMH staff member can be an important source of information and has direct links to provincial organizations that are responsible for methadone treatment in Ontario.

The first meeting

The first meeting is a critical step for establishing a working group and lays the groundwork for successful community collaboration. It gives you the opportunity to educate potential members of the working group and to learn from them. Pre-meeting preparation and skillful meeting facilitation will ensure you achieve the objectives of the meeting.

"Put a lot of effort into meeting management, such as group facilitation, well-prepared documentation, staying on time and smart goal-setting. A working group that enjoys working together ends up working well together."

—*MMT case manager*

Generally, the objectives of the first meeting are to:
· review and discuss the needs of the community
· educate the participants
· listen and learn from the participants
· establish consensus
· determine the members of the working group
· draft the next steps.

TIP ▷

Videoconferencing or teleconferencing may be a useful meeting tool for communities that have a widespread population and encompass a large geographic area.

Before the meeting

There is a lot to get done at the first meeting. Thorough pre-meeting planning and preparation can help ensure the first meeting runs as smoothly as possible. Before the meeting:

Define the initiative and the purpose of the meeting

While you were talking with each of the invitees, you likely refined and polished how you described the initiative. Use this honed description to define the purpose of the first meeting.

The meeting's purpose should clearly focus on exploring the needs of the community and people who are dependent on opioids.

· Draft an outline of what you hope to achieve at the first meeting.
· Summarize the main points into a brief list of meeting objectives.

Refine your needs assessment findings

Since drafting your needs assessment report, you may have also discovered new information to add to it. Summarize your findings in a format that can be read at-a-glance. A more detailed version can be included in your meeting handouts. Highlight local information as much as possible. Use provincial and national information to support the local findings.

Identify the knowledge gaps

Your discussions with community partners will have also helped identify the gaps in the community's knowledge of MMT. Tailor the education part of your presentation to address these gaps in understanding and to correct any misconceptions.

· Know the history of MMT in the community.
· Be aware of the community's level of awareness and acceptance, and its motivation to support or oppose the initiative.
· Focus on best practices of MMT delivery, for example offering counselling and health and social support services.

The education part of the meeting can be delivered by one or a combination of the following methods:

· the meeting leader
· guest speaker (see below)
· *Prescription for Addiction* DVD.

PRESCRIPTION FOR ADDICTION DVD

Laura Sky, producer
David Adkin, director and editor

Prescription for Addiction is a compelling documentary that examines the growing problem of dependence and addiction to opioid pain medications. This DVD includes insights from clients, family members, doctors and other health care professionals. It comes with a comprehensive *User Guide* offering support for facilitators, teachers and others wishing to screen the film in their communities.

It was produced by Sky Works Charitable Foundation and commissioned by CAMH, in partnership with the Ontario Federation of Community Mental Health and Addiction Programs and St. Joseph's Health Care Group, Thunder Bay.

For more information, visit: http://www.camh.net/Care_Treatment/ Program_Descriptions/opiate/Prescription_for_Addiction_Kit.html.

Enlist the support of a guest speaker

You may choose to enlist the services of a guest speaker or speakers to deliver the education portion of the meeting. The guest speaker should be a persuasive presenter who can support the program in a way that resonates with your particular community. Their presentation should underline MMT's efficacy, demonstrate successes of this type of treatment in other communities and emphasize the need for MMT in your community. Potential guest speakers include:

· client or family member of a client, or someone from the community or another community who can demonstrate the efficacy of MMT with first-hand experience

- working group member from another community that implemented a successful MMT program
- subject-matter expert, such as an MMT physician or other respected member of the provincial groups responsible for the quality and accessibility of MMT in Ontario, for example the CPSO or CAMH.

TIP ▷   **Support your supporters. Prepare and inform your guest speakers before the meeting, giving them clear information about what you would like them to speak about. Make sure they have been told what they can expect and what type of questions or issues may come up. Be sure to also offer them support during and after the meeting.**

Prepare handouts

Prepare clear, easy-to-read handouts that the participants can refer to for more in-depth information about MMT and the initiative. Handouts:
- reinforce the information presented during the meeting
- help participants retain information and facts correctly
- help you to support the supporters by giving them consistent messaging and information to share with others.

Participants of the first meeting may use these handouts to inform their colleagues and neighbours about the initiative. Keep your messaging consistent and suitable for a wider audience, including opponents. Include relevant Internet addresses for further reading.

TIP ▷   **CAMH has a wealth of resources (print and online) for the general public and for health care professionals that you can use to support your awareness and education efforts. Visit http://methadonesaves-lives.ca and see *Resources* on page 93.**

Appoint a meeting leader and note-taker

Other people who can help you with the first meeting include:
- meeting leader: You may choose to facilitate the meeting yourself or invite someone else to run the meeting. It can be helpful to hire an experienced, third-party facilitator to keep the meeting on track. This can be particularly useful if you predict emotions will run high at the first meeting.
- note-taker: Appoint a skilled note-taker to record accurately the minutes of the meeting.

Create and practise your presentation

The initial meeting is not a place to show off your expertise. Your presentation should be persuasive, but as succinct as possible. Highlight the key messages.

Your presentation should include:
· meeting agenda
· outline of the objectives of the meeting
· summary of the needs assessment
· group education, delivered by yourself, meeting leader, guest speaker or DVD.

Practise your presentation, especially if you are presenting it yourself. Be sure to check beforehand that the equipment (e.g., computer, projector, lights) in the meeting room is working properly.

During the meeting

The initial meeting is a large undertaking that requires skillful facilitation. While educating the working group is an important part of the meeting, remember that everyone will be eager to share their knowledge, experience and opinions. Be mindful of the time, stick to the agenda and maintain as much structure as possible to keep the meeting moving forward and to achieve the objectives.

Adhere to the agenda

Set a meeting agenda and stick to it as closely as possible. In today's world, everyone is very busy. Running an efficient meeting will show that you respect the participants' time and value their participation.

State the meeting's purpose and your expectations

Clearly state what you hope to achieve. Share with the group your draft outline of the objectives of the meeting. Ask them if they have anything to add or revise.

Educate the group

Educating the group is an essential component of the initial meeting. In the meeting planning stages, you will have prepared a presentation tailored to the educational needs of the group. Remember, this is the information the meeting attendees will take back to the community.

· Support your presentation with printed handouts and resources.
· Discuss the proven efficacy of methadone treatment.
· Focus on the needs of the community (the findings of your community needs assessment report).

Review needs assessment

Present the needs assessment report, highlighting the information that shows a clear need to develop methadone treatment services in the community. Remember, assessing the needs of the community is an ongoing process. The first meeting of the working group will likely add more information to the report. Completing the needs assessment may be the first objective for forming the working group.

Invite and facilitate discussion

Reporting the needs assessment findings will inevitably lead to group discussion. It is likely that everyone has experience, ideas and opinions they would like to share. Discuss their ideas and viewpoints. While it is valuable to let everyone have a chance to speak, it is equally important to be respectful of people's time and ensure that the meeting keeps moving.

Helpful reminders during open discussion:
· avoid allowing one person to dominate the conversation
· address opposing views
· stick to the meeting's purpose and stay focussed on the agenda
· focus on the needs of the clients.

Be prepared to deal with conflict

Some of the discussion may become heated, especially if you have invited opponents of the initiative to the meeting. During your needs assessment research, you will likely have gathered information that will foreshadow the type of objections you may encounter. Be prepared with facts and research.

You may consider inviting subject-matter experts to the meeting to deal with these issues, such as a physician or other professional already working with methadone clients or representatives from CAMH or CPSO.

They will be able to offer counterarguments founded on evidence-based research and clinical practice. Clients and members of their family can also offer valuable first-hand testimonials to help deal with conflict. Their stories often illustrate very clearly the benefits of MMT, help debunk myths and misconceptions and underline the need. (See *Troubleshooting* on page 50.)

> *"Be respectful of difference. People may be at different points in their understanding and beliefs about MMT. What everyone has in common is a concern about the issue."*
>
> —CAMH *program consultant*

Doctors who already provide MMT in your area or in another community can help raise awareness and acceptance among the attendees to the first meeting of the working group. A physician supporter, or champion of the cause, can also diffuse challenges and offer personal accounts of their experience.

◁ TIP

Establish consensus

Following open discussion, bring the group back to the meeting's objectives and work towards establishing consensus. One of the best ways to establish a consensus is to focus on the needs of the clients. The first goal of the meeting is to educate. The education portion of the meeting will hopefully encourage attendees to agree that MMT is an effective treatment option for many opioid users. Consensus may simply be that the attendees agree to meet again to explore further whether or not to establish new or expand existing MMT services.

> *"Don't rush the process. Building consensus takes time."*
>
> —CAMH *program consultant*

Outline the next steps

Before adjourning the meeting, outline the next steps for the working group. These may include:
· appointment of various duties, such as a chairperson, secretary and media spokesperson
· priorities
· general time line
· date of the next meeting.

The working group should collectively choose a chairperson or group leader for the subsequent meetings of the working group. The chairperson is responsible for setting meeting dates, planning agendas, preparing minutes and facilitating meetings. Ensure you have the administrative support for the meetings, especially note-taking. It is also advisable to consider who will be the group's media spokesperson.

Sustain the community working group

Being part of a working group involves a sustained commitment from each of the members. Members should feel that they are part of a group that is affecting positive change in the community. Here are some tips for maintaining an effective working group.

· Clearly define the purpose of the working group.
· Outline the duties and expectations for each member.
· Hold meetings often enough to continue the momentum.
· Support the meetings with good communication.
· Ensure that the next steps are always clear.
· Be respectful of people's time and opinions.
· Celebrate successes (even small ones).

A Mother's Story

My son died from an opioid overdose. Since his death, I continue to fight for effective treatments and options. To see my son struggle with and eventually die from opioid drug addiction has been the most devastating experience of my life. We could not find effective help for my son. I know that, had there been a MMT program available for Pete, he would be alive today.

I believe strongly that effective care and choice are fundamental human rights for all addicts who genuinely want out. Each and every one deserves that opportunity, regardless of social status or lack of money. They are the experts of their own lives and are best equipped to decide what treatment option could potentially save their lives and make them healthier sooner.

Sharing my son's story to raise awareness, educate, reduce stigma and doing my part to help secure funding for an MMT program in my community helps me to re-invest in life. By intentionally redirecting the focus from the systemic failures as they applied to my son and refocusing my efforts to help change attitudes is empowering. Encouraging acceptance and openness to an effective harm reduction initiative—the MMT program—invites everyone in the community to be part of the solution.

I am a bereaved mother who can break down rigid, closed mindsets that are often based in bold prejudice, unsubstantiated fear or lack of knowledge. Telling my story touches people and allows them to emotionally connect. They realize that this program could very well save the life of one of their own children or loved one!

That is why I am involved with my community's MMT [Planning] Committee—for myself, for others and on behalf of and in memory of my son.

Engaging the community

While you don't need community approval and participation to open an MMT clinic, experience shows that educating and engaging the community early on in the process promotes awareness and acceptance of the benefits of treating opioid dependence. Having the support of the community can help ensure the success of an effective treatment program.

To educate and engage the wider community, the working group should first develop a community awareness and outreach strategy. This section offers suggestions that can be adapted to create an awareness outreach strategy that fits your community's needs and resources.

Determine your awareness outreach goals

First, the working group should determine and prioritize the goals of your community awareness and outreach strategy. The main goal of your strategy is to establish two-way communication with the community. Your awareness and outreach strategy should also:

Advocate openness
Show the community that you have an organized consultation process and that community input is an important part of the development, implementation and evaluation of MMT services. Do not give the community the sense that the project is a "done deal."

"There was no opportunity for community discussion, consultation or input. They should have at least had a meeting where community members could have met the operators and discussed concerns. Such efforts of advance firefighting might have been seen as a positive move."
—citizen from a community that was not consulted

It has been the experience of several communities in Ontario that community consultation and acceptance of a program plan before MMT services are set up for operation can diffuse or even avoid community opposition.
· Engage the community proactively and early on in the development process.
· Show how the project contributes positively to the community.
· Share the results of your community needs assessment.

"The solution to opioid dependence problems in a community is not just the responsibility of physicians, or the addiction agencies, or the hospital, or community agencies. It is everybody's responsibility to come together to help people who have this problem, not just because it's the right thing to do for that individual, but because it's the right thing to do for the community."
—physician, addiction specialist

Reduce stigma
As mentioned earlier, opposition often stems from prejudice and fears about people who are dependent on opioids. (See *What to expect* on page 21.) One of the main goals of your outreach strategy will be to reduce the stigma surrounding people who are opioid dependent.

Fears are often based on lack of knowledge. Many people have a pre-conceived picture of people who are dependent on opioids. The truth is that opioid dependency can happen to anyone.
· Educate the community about the diversity of people who are dependent on opioids.
· Introduce the community to real client stories.
· Address any fears people may voice.

"There is no typical injection drug user. Especially with opioids, it's right across the whole spectrum."

—*street-wise harm reduction worker*

Dispel myths about MMT

Along with giving a face to the people who want treatment for their opioid dependence, help dispel the myths about MMT. Focus on the successes of delivering well-planned methadone treatment services suited to the community rather than merely describing how methadone works pharmacologically.

· Improve the community's understanding of the treatment options for opioid dependency.

· Increase awareness of the benefits of MMT.

· Initiate greater awareness around prescription opioid dependency.

New research from CAMH shows a dramatic increase in the number of people seeking detoxification treatment for opioid dependence. Surprisingly, the cause of this increase is the use of prescription pain medication, not heroin. Published in *Canadian Family Physician* (January 2009), the CAMH study found that, of the people coming to the Medical Withdrawal Service of CAMH for the treatment of opioid dependence, those having a problem with OxyContin increased steadily from fewer than 4% to 55% over a five-year period (Sproule et al., 2009).

◄ QUICK FACT

"Naturally, communities are concerned about issues of open drug use that create unsafe neighbourhoods. Methadone offers a solution to these issues."

—*community health centre director*

Gain acceptance

An informed community that is aware of the benefits of MMT is more likely to accept the introduction or expansion of MMT services in their neighbourhood. Gaining a community's acceptance and support will help ensure the success of the project.

· Show how an MMT program can be integrated positively into the community.

· Tailor the information to the needs and goals of the community (e.g., MMT can reduce HIV/HVC rates and drug use, prevent crime).

· Promote a collaborative, coordinated model of care with your service partners and community.
· Address fears people may have (e.g., depreciation of or safety in their neighbourhood).

"People who attend MMT clinics want to change their lifestyle. That's why they are participating."

—*MMT case manager*

Develop your awareness outreach strategy

There is no "one-size-fits-all" awareness outreach strategy. Exactly when and how the public should be consulted will vary from community to community. For example, you may choose to engage the community once you have finalized the needs assessment and drafted your action plan—a job that can take months to complete. Other communities may decide to consult members of the community before the action plan is finished.

Pooling information from the needs assessment and individual experiences of the working group members can start to give you an idea of the community's level of awareness and acceptance of MMT. Tailor your outreach strategy to suit this awareness and acceptance level. You should also consider other challenges specific to your community.

· Population base: Is your community widespread or in a concentrated urban area?
· Language and/or culture: What languages, Aboriginal or ethnocultural communities do you need to include in your strategy approach?

The next challenge is to get your information out to the community and put your strategy into action.

Put your strategy into action

These strategy approaches were drawn from the experience of working groups who have successfully developed MMT services in their communities. Adapt these approaches to meet the goals of your awareness outreach strategy. Similarly, you may wish to contact working groups of other communities to learn from their experiences and how they put their strategy into action.

Hold information sessions

Community outreach and awareness education often involves public information sessions or meetings. Review the presentation you used to educate the working group to see which parts you may be able to repurpose for the wider community. (See *Before the meeting* on page 32.)

You will likely hold several information sessions for various groups of the community, such as the general public, community leaders, local politicians, local business owners or health care providers. (See *Recruit service providers* on page 58.) Tailor each information session to the specific audience.

"You know, it's all about education and people are not being educated. And it's all about communication. Without knowing the facts [about MMT services], people are getting all upset ... believing that everything is going to hell in a hand basket. But that's not the case."
— *community liaison police officer*

Have an onsite counsellor available at the information meetings to offer support to any participants who may need help dealing with emotions or issues that come up.

◁ TIP

There are a number of presentation approaches you can use to educate your audience.

· Ask a client or family member of a client to tell their story and discuss their first-hand experience with opioid addiction and MMT.
· Have a working group member from another community that implemented a successful MMT program talk about their experience.
· Engage a subject-matter expert from the working group or from a provincial body, such as CAMH or CPSO.
· Invite a member of the working group to present at meetings of their peers and colleagues.
· Show and discuss the documentary *Prescription for Addiction*. The companion *User Guide* gives detailed information on how to advertise a showing of the documentary as well as how you can show it in segments and engage the audience in discussion.

TIP ▷

Even if you decide not to show the documentary *Prescription for Addiction,* consult the companion *User Guide* for detailed information on promoting your event and facilitating discussion. The guide also offers valuable support materials and frequently asked questions about opioid dependence and addiction. Download a copy of the *User Guide* from the Methadone Saves Lives website at http://methadonesaveslives.ca.

Educate and engage community leaders

Local support or opposition for the project will be shaped by community leaders. Reach out to the leaders in your community.

Community leaders may include:
· elected officials, such as the city councillor, MP and MPP and, if applicable, the band chief, band councillor and elders
· the chair of community groups, residents' or ratepayers' associations, business improvement or business development groups
· representatives of local community centres and cultural centres
· representatives of community agencies, such as public health units, needle exchange programs, addiction treatment providers, mental health agencies, harm reduction programs, AIDS organizations and social services departments
· medical officer of health
· members of the medical community
· local school principals and board members
· local religious leaders
· members of the local police department or correction services
· editors of local newspapers, representatives from local radio and television stations.

Educate the community leaders by inviting them to attend information sessions. Engage them by asking them to form an advisory committee to support the efforts of the working group.

HALTON: A COMMUNITY ENGAGEMENT SUCCESS STORY

Upon completing their needs assessment and action plan, the Halton MMT community working group presented their program plan to local politicians and the Halton Health and Social Services Committee. Local supporters—an MMT client and a mother whose son died of an overdose because there was no program to help him with his addiction to prescription opioids—delivered compelling presentations underlying the need for MMT services in the Halton area with their personal stories.

The working group was able to secure full support of the attendees. Media coverage of the event was very positive and led the way to educating and engaging the wider community.

Organize an advisory committee of community members

Members of the community may wish to be actively involved in the development and implementation of MMT services in their neighbourhood. Invite them to be part of an advisory committee or community liaison group. A community advisory committee can:
· be a liaison between the community and the working group
· foster community acceptance and support
· review and provide feedback on the action plan
· help execute the plan
· participate in monitoring and evaluating the program.

Make the most of your champions

While establishing the working group, you identified supporters, or champions of the cause. Champions are often members of the community who have a strong personal, community or professional link to opioid dependence. Their compelling first-hand stories about opioid dependency and conviction about the efficacy and need for MMT in the community can be a powerful outreach tool.

Champions may be:
· MMT clients or family members of a client
· potential client or family members of someone who would benefit from MMT were it available in the community

· members of the working group (perhaps someone who initially was opposed to the initiative)
· influential community leaders
· MMT subject-matter experts from the community, such as MMT physicians
· MMT physicians from a nearby community.

Champions can:
· make presentations at public information meetings
· participate in interviews with the media
· tell their story for written communications (press releases, hand-outs, web pages, etc.)
· write letters of support.

"A champion who speaks from experience is able to move people from their heads to their hearts."

—*CAMH program consultant*

Contact the media
The media may only take notice of the project when there is a problem. Proactively contacting the local media is a productive and inexpensive way to positively promote and publicize the project plan and educate the public. Be sure to also contact the media of local Aboriginal and ethnocultural groups.

To encourage positive press coverage, you can:
· prepare media information kits
· write press releases for local media
· send a well-prepared spokesperson to media interviews
· invite the media to your information sessions.

When dealing with the media, describe the benefits of MMT clearly and simply for the layperson. (See *What are the benefits of MMT?* on page 9.) Make sure your key messages and awareness strategy goals are covered in the news stories.

Refer to methadone as a medication to help shift popular public opinion that methadone simply substitutes one drug for another. For example, you can say: *"Methadone is a prescription medication. It is part of a long-term treatment for people dependent on opioids."*

Written materials

Written materials help support your awareness outreach efforts. They ensure that your key messages and MMT information and facts are conveyed consistently and remembered correctly. Written materials can include:
· flyer-style invitations to information sessions
· frequently-asked-questions documents
· information brochures, booklets, Internet resources
· letters
· press releases.

All written materials should be cleanly designed and easy to read. If possible, offer translated versions of your written materials in the languages most often spoken in the community. Be sure to include a one-page document among your information materials that outlines:
· who you are
· what you propose
· what opportunities there are for community input
· how to contact you.

CAMH, and possibly your local addiction and mental health agencies, can supply handouts about opioid dependency and MMT that you can use. These include brochures, booklets and web resources. (Visit Methadone Save Lives at http://methadonesaveslives.ca and see *Resources* on page 93 for useful written material that you may wish to use.)

"It is always important to be as comprehensive as possible when putting together any literature for the public."

—*MMT program director*

Troubleshooting

Even with the most well-directed awareness efforts, you may still face challenging questions and objections from some members of the community. These objections may be rooted in ignorance, fear and bias that you can respond to and often disprove with research and fact.

Here are some of the most commonly heard objections and a succinct response to each. You can also find additional supportive information, facts and research in *About methadone maintenance treatment* on page 5. You may not have the chance to give all the facts at a public meeting; sometimes people are too angry or upset to listen. Be sure to include the most important information in your written materials.

Why would you want to give drug users more drugs?
Methadone is a prescription medication. It is part of a long-term treatment for people who are dependent on opioids. Opioid dependence is a medical disorder. People who are dependent on opioids deserve treatment as much as any other person who has a medical disorder.

The perceived risk that MMT may maintain people in an addicted lifestyle is simply not supported by research. Methadone is currently the most effective treatment currently available for opioid dependence. The success of any MMT program is improved by directing attention to the quality of treatment and supporting that treatment with counselling and appropriate health and social support services. Our project outlines a quality treatment model based on our community's available resources and client needs.

Why don't they just stop using?
No one intends to develop an opioid dependence problem. Some people use opioids for the first time when they were prescribed by a doctor to treat pain for a physical injury from a workplace or car accident. While there are people who may be able to stop using drugs on their own, others need help dealing with opioid dependence. It is often thought that opioid drug dependence is self-inflicted and efforts to treat people who are dependent on opioids will inevitably fail. Not so. Opioid dependence is a brain-related medical disorder for which there are effective treatments. A community like ours should make sure that treatment options, such as MMT, are available and accessible for people seeking help.

This isn't the best way to care for people who are dependent on opioids.

The experts would disagree with you. Hundreds of clinical studies and reports, including the *Ontario Report of the Methadone Maintenance Treatment Practices Task Force* and the *Clinical Practice Guidelines* from the College of Physicians and Surgeons of Ontario, speak of the benefits of MMT.

Methadone is the most effective treatment currently available for opioid dependence. It has been rigorously studied and has yielded the best results. MMT benefits not only the people receiving treatment, but also their families, their community and society as a whole. Medically supervised methadone treatment works best when combined with health and social support. Our project includes integrated support services. (See *About methadone maintenance treatment* on page 5 for more supporting facts.)

Why can't these people go somewhere else?

Like you and me, people who are dependent on opioids have the right to receive medical treatment in their community, close to where they live. Why should they have to travel to other communities to get the care and support they need?

If we start a methadone program in our community, won't all the drug users move into this area?

Our needs assessment shows that we have people in our community right now who would benefit from MMT and support services. The people in our community who are treating and managing their opioid dependency are currently travelling outside of the community to get treatment. People rarely disclose that they are dependent on opioids because there is so much stigma associated with it. With effective MMT services in the community, your friends, family members, neighbours and other potential MMT clients will get the treatment and support they need.

When you bring in problem people, you get problem neighbourhoods.

The problem is not the people but rather that people who are dependent on opioids lack treatment options and aren't getting appropriate health and social support services. And these problems can become neighbourhood problems if people can't get the care they need from qualified health care professionals. Problems are not created by good treatment options and support services such as the ones we propose—they are solved by them.

You're trying to sneak this project through without consulting the community.

Actually, we are judiciously consulting the community, offering information sessions and opportunities for feedback, such as this meeting. We advocate openness and encourage members of the community to become involved in the planning and development process.

What benefit would this be to the community? ("Crime is going to increase. Our neighbourhood won't be safe anymore.")

MMT promotes health, reduces the criminal behaviour associated with illegal drug use and improves social productivity. Opioid users may turn to criminal activity to feed their habit. They may be involved in the legal, court, corrections systems and they or their dependents may need social assistance, all of which bear high societal costs. Following a comprehensive MMT program as our project recommends, clients can stabilize their lives improve their overall social functioning and quality of life. We believe that the plan we have proposed is well-designed and will add value to the community. (See *Cost benefits and cost effectiveness* on page 12 for more supportive information.)

What if someone tries to sell the methadone or abuses the program?

While we cannot control people's behaviours, studies show that providing a comprehensive MMT program along with counselling and health and social support services, as outlined in our project, yields the best results. Methadone is the most effective treatment currently available for opioid dependence.

One risk of treatment is the diversion of drugs to the black market. However, this risk can be reduced and treatment benefits increased by directing attention to the quality of treatment (Bell & Zador, 2000).

Clients seeking treatment are motivated to make a positive change to their quality of life. MMT along with social supports helps clients stabilize their lives and break the negative patterns of an addiction lifestyle, such as seeking illicit drugs and turning to illegal methods of making money to pay for street drugs.

Is our community able to meet the needs of all methadone patients?
We believe the rigor that was used to develop our project considers the needs of our community's methadone clients and potential clients as well as the resources of the community. Our action plan also includes ongoing monitoring and evaluation of the services and community consultation, which will help identify and address any potential service gaps in the model.

Pete's Story

My son Pete was addicted to oxycodone opioid pain medications (Percocet and OxyContin). He died of an overdose of these drugs when he was 25 years old.

Pete was an intelligent, articulate young man struggling with depression and crushing anxiety. He had the full support of his family and his friends. This sensitive, loving and entertaining kid, who had a deep desire to accomplish something great in his lifetime, fell into the trap of escaping the pain and confusion through self medication.

Pete's addiction started innocently enough when he was prescribed opioid painkillers for gastrointestinal flare-ups. But the prescribed treatment soon morphed into a trap that consumed him. In addition to medicating his physical pain, the drugs also medicated his emotional and mental pain. He often described the "perfect" high as one that energized him and relieved his depression. The addiction ravaged his psyche and the constant need for more grew.

He couldn't just stop...even when he desperately wanted to. The physical withdrawal symptoms made it impossible for him to stop using. As Pete spiralled out of control, we both became terrified. I was terrified for him and Pete was fast becoming more terrified of living than dying. My worst fears came true on December 23, 2001, when my son died.

Had an MMT program been available for Pete, I know unequivocally that he would be here today as proof positive of the ability of methadone to significantly change the lives of a lot of people. He could not access MMT—this gift of life—and now he symbolizes what happens when methadone treatment is not available.

This can happen to anyone and we need to rid society of the stereotype that only people lacking character and willpower can succumb to such an illness.

Developing a methadone maintenance treatment program

The minimum services required to operate an MMT program are physicians, pharmacists and laboratory services. Research shows that adding counselling services and health and social support services to the program increases the likelihood of positive outcomes to your program's treatment goals. These outcomes include improved client physical and psychological health and better quality of life as well as long-term benefits for society, such as reduced rates of crime and lower social and economic costs.

Define goals and identify resources and barriers

The goal of every community is to design a collaborative, coordinated model of care that will best meet clients' needs and add value to the community. Exactly how this is done varies widely from community to community. (See *How is MMT delivered?* on page 13 for more information on MMT delivery models.)

> *"Consult with MMT programs that have a similar mandate or model to the direction your community would like to take. There are great people out there doing great work in MMT. Most are happy to talk about their programs. Make good use of these folks."*
> —CAMH *program consultant*

Start by clearly defining the goals of your program. These goals should balance the treatment goals and needs of your clients, service providers and the community along with the available resources and potential barriers.

Assess the resources and potential barriers in your community that will shape your MMT program model. These include:
· client and community needs
· service provider awareness and acceptance of MMT
· physician, pharmacist and laboratory services involvement
· participation of community health and social support services
· partnering opportunities
· financial resources.

Consider client and community needs

Focus first on the needs and treatment goals of the clients. The primary goal of any MMT program is to improve clients' health and quality of life. If your program cannot meet these treatment goals and needs of the clients, the full benefits to the client and the community cannot be realized.

People who are dependent on opioids are a diverse population with many reasons for seeking treatment. While most will benefit from counselling, they do not all have the same type or level of need for additional supportive services. For example, some may need shelter, food, child care or financial support, while others may not. Many clients also need support stabilizing and rebuilding family relationships through services such as marriage/relationship counselling, parent and family counselling and assistance in dealing with child welfare agencies.

If a client's needs are not met, then their ability to stay in treatment may be jeopardized. Therefore, the services of the program model should be suitably varied and flexible and be able to respond to the needs of clients, their severity of dependence, personal circumstances, motivation and response to treatment.

Furthermore, there are some clients who have special treatment issues that require specific health and social supports. These include:
· people with polysubstance-use behaviours
· women
· women who are pregnant
· youth
· homeless persons

- people living in rural or remote areas
- First Nations, Métis and Inuit clients
- people living with HCV
- people living with HIV/AIDS
- people living with mental health disorders
- offenders in the corrections system.

> **Research shows that combining counselling with MMT improves treatment outcomes and should be considered an essential component of methadone treatment programs (Wilson et al., 2007; Gossop et al., 2003; Callaly et al., 2001).**

◀ QUICK FACT

Develop a comprehensive MMT program model that includes access to community health and social support services. This will require agreements with the partner agencies and clear referral protocols, procedures and policies. (See *Policies and procedures* on page 73.) Community health and social support services may include counselling, case management, mental health services, health promotion, disease prevention and education and other community-based services, such as legal, financial, medical, child care, dental and housing services. (See *Components of an MMT program* on page 15.)

> *"It is fundamental that methadone maintenance treatment be integrated into a wider scope of services."*
>
> —*MMT case manager*

Design your model to be a client-centred program that:
- is easily accessible
- recognizes and accepts that every client enters treatment with widely varying experiences, expectations and needs
- respects clients' dignity
- fosters a collaborative, relationship-building approach between clients and program team members
- tailors treatment to meet individual clients' needs
- outlines clearly articulated rules that are followed consistently.

CLIENT PEER SUPPORT

Consider including a client peer support element to your program. Peers can help spread the word about the program and its benefits to potential clients. They can inform new clients about the program and its services. They can also encourage each other at various points throughout their care continuum. Peers are especially valuable to clients who are in crisis.

Using peer support promotes client involvement in the clinic and the community. They can meet regularly to address issues that may arise concerning the clinic, the services or other aspects of the program. Furthermore, peers can be instrumental in raising awareness in the community and supporting recruitment of service providers. They should be encouraged to tell their stories (Hart, 2007; Wilson et al., 2007).

Clients who offer support to their peers should be trained and receive on-going support and guidance from the appropriate counselling professionals in the program.

Recruit service providers

Recruiting health care providers and partnering with community support services are challenging tasks of the development stage. Involve service providers as early on in the program development process as possible. While the model of care should focus on the needs of the clients, you must also consider the needs and resources of the service providers to have an effective, collaborative program.

QUICK FACT ▶ **Too many people (service providers included) see opioid addiction as a self-inflicted disease of the will. They believe that a drug-free state is the only acceptable goal and that any attempt at treatment will inevitably fail. However, opioid drug addictions can indeed be effectively treated with significant benefits to the individual and to society (NIH Consensus Conference, 1998).**

Recruitment of service providers will involve breaking down biases and stereotypes and correcting misconceptions. You should educate potential service providers by engaging them in awareness outreach activities.

To raise awareness and gain acceptance of MMT, you can:
· hold information sessions, including arranging in-service presentations
· prepare service provider-specific handouts
  (See http://methadonesaveslives.ca.)
· enlist the support of guest speakers (e.g., peers, clients or subject-matter experts)

> *"...addiction is a very marginalized illness. Society doesn't understand it very well. Doctors don't understand it very well. To bring it out into the open as an illness that is [treatable] ...would be wonderful."*
> *—family physician and MMT prescriber*

Revise the presentation you made to the working group to suit the specific service-provider audience. (See *The first meeting* on page 31.) Information sessions may be given to groups or in a one-on-one setting. The education portion of the meeting could be presented by a physician or other health care professional experienced in methadone treatment. You may also wish to partner with related organizations and associations to educate and recruit service providers, for example:
· CAMH
· CPSO
· local medical school
· local medical society
· community health centres
· emergency department
· local pharmacy association
· local network of addiction agencies
· LHIN.

Doctors who already provide MMT in your area or in another community can help raise awareness and acceptance among potential service providers. A physician supporter, or champion of the cause, can help educate and recruit.

◁ TIP

These organizations and associations can help your education and recruitment efforts. They may be able to:
· hold methadone information sessions in conjunction with their regularly scheduled association meetings
· endorse information sessions or meetings that you host
· send out invitations to the meeting to their members, using their letterhead or e-mail
· send out follow-up information
· give you a list of their members
· provide guest speaker(s) for information sessions
· provide honorariums for client and family speakers.

Recruitment of service providers, especially physician and pharmacists, is often an ongoing effort. Having them help shape your program model is ideal. However, you may need to continue recruiting after you have decided on a program model. You may find that some physicians and other service providers may be willing to join the program only once you have community acceptance of the project plan.

Similarly, some (especially physicians) may join the team after program elements have been established, for example a program site, access to case management and counselling services, administrative support, links to health and social support services. Service providers joining the program later in the development process may offer additional infrastructure or service delivery components that will modify the program model.

MMT POLICY CHANGES IN CANADA

Given the proven benefits of MMT, the following policy changes were made in 1996 in Canada to improve access to this effective treatment option for opioid dependency and to ease the shortage of physicians and other health care providers who can deliver MMT (Fischer et al., 2002, Strike et al., 2005).
· Regulatory oversight was transferred from the federal government to the provinces.
· Administration became the responsibility of the Colleges of Physicians and Surgeons.

Continued on page 61

MMT Policy Changes in Canada...Continued from page 60

· Treatment guidelines were revised.
· Caseload limits were rescinded.
· Training requirements were shortened.

Physicians

Physicians are an imperative component to any MMT service delivery model. Without them, a program cannot be established. They are responsible for the prescription of methadone treatment and all attending liabilities. Physicians must be approved by Health Canada, on the recommendation of their provincial regulatory body, and receive an exemption to be able to prescribe methadone for opioid addiction. In Ontario, this requires the completion of approved training offered by CAMH. (See *Training for service providers* on page 72.)

CAMH'S OPIOID DEPENDENCE TREATMENT CERTIFICATE PROGRAM

The interprofessional *Opioid Dependence Treatment Certificate Program* prepares physicians, pharmacists, nurses and counsellors to assess and treat people with opioid dependence. The core course meets the CPSO and OCP regulatory requirements for prescribing and dispensing methadone and buprenorphine for treatment of opioid dependence. Participants receive relevant continuing education credits upon completion of the course.

The program uses a blended-learning approach that includes online and classroom components. Participants are required to complete:
· core course: five self-directed online modules followed by a one-day workshop
· elective courses: three or four elective courses.

Contact CAMH for more details and upcoming course dates. See *Resources* on page 93 for more information.

To recruit physicians, you can:
· get a list of local doctors from your local medical societies, LHIN or a physician contact
· contact the CPSO for guidance and support on physician recruitment
· invite physicians to an information session
· seek endorsements from the LHIN and the local medical society
· enlist a subject-matter expert to facilitate the meeting
· invite other appropriate supporters to make presentations at the meeting, such as practising MMT peers, clients, members of the working group, CPSO representatives
· set up one-on-one meetings with individual physicians or physician cooperatives
· show the documentary *Prescription for Addiction* (DVD)
· present clinical research and support materials about MMT, its benefits, your project and the physician exemption and training requirements
· supply attendees with contact information for the working group, CPSO and CAMH where they can get more information
· arrange to have an MMT physician speak during grand rounds at the local hospital.

Doctors who already provide MMT in your area or in another community can help raise awareness and acceptance among local doctors about the program model and its related benefits. A physician supporter can also help educate and recruit other service providers, such as pharmacists, nurses, nurse practitioners, related health care providers and counsellors.

> *"Be patient but persistent. You only have to engage one or two physicians in order to get the clinic started. All of our physicians were recruited by a physician already prescribing methadone."*
> —MMT *program director*

Ideally, your community should have more than one MMT doctor so that they can support one another and provide consistent care in the case of illness, vacations and out-of-town commitments. If you cannot successfully recruit a physician, you may invite an MMT physician from another community to assist temporarily until a physician from within the community can be recruited.

"The mandate of CPSO's program to improve the quality and accessibility of MMT in Ontario is achieved in cooperation with CAMH and OCP. The profile of methadone treatment in Ontario has been enhanced through outreach activities and the recruitment of physicians to prescribe methadone in the treatment of opioid dependence."

—*CPSO website*

Pharmacists

Community pharmacists are also essential service providers for an MMT model. Any pharmacy can dispense methadone provided that the methadone policy outlined by OCP is followed. Methadone training through CAMH's *Opioid Dependence Treatment Certificate Program* or approved course is highly recommended for all pharmacists and is required for the pharmacy manager and at least one staff pharmacist.

The decision whether or not to dispense methadone is entirely the choice of the pharmacist or pharmacy owner. Your recruitment goals will include increasing awareness and acceptance of your program among your community's pharmacists and owners or designated managers of the local pharmacies.

To recruit pharmacists, you can:
· get a list of local pharmacists from the local pharmacist association or pharmacist contact
· invite pharmacists to an information session
· ask for support from pharmacist associations, such as the OCP and the Ontario Pharmacists' Association (OPA)
· enlist a subject-matter expert to facilitate the meeting
· invite other appropriate supporters to make presentations at the meeting, such as other pharmacists who dispense methadone, an MMT physician, and clients and members of the working group
· show the documentary *Prescription for Addiction* (DVD)
· present clinical research and support materials about MMT, its benefits, your project and training opportunities
· supply attendees with contact information for the working group, OCP, OPA and CAMH where they can get more information

· ask physicians involved in the program to help recruit pharmacists with whom they work closely
· set up one-on-one meetings with individual pharmacists or staff of pharmacies.

QUICK FACT ▶

The Ontario College of Pharmacists published their updated *Policy for Dispensing Methadone* in 2006. All Ontario pharmacists dispensing methadone are required to follow the policy. See www.ocpinfo.com for more information.

Laboratory Services

Laboratory services are also an important component of the model, primarily providing collection and analysis of urine samples. Your recruitment should start with the laboratories that your physicians work with. Invite laboratory owners to information sessions to dispel any stigma and raise awareness and acceptance of the MMT program.

Case Managers and Counsellors

Case managers and counsellors are an integral part of an MMT program. They provide support and ongoing assessment and adjustment of a client's treatment program. They also link clients to the health and social support services they may need. CAMH's interprofessional *Opioid Dependence Treatment Certificate Program* is recommended for counsellors.

To recruit case managers and counsellors, you can:
· partner with addiction treatment agencies or other community support services to share case management and counselling loads
· seek funding to hire case managers and counsellors for the program. (See *Secure resources and funding* on page 66.)

"Addiction counselling is really important."
                              —*family physician and MMT prescriber*

Nurses and nurse practitioners

Nurses and nurse practitioners are sometimes included in MMT care team. Depending on the service delivery model their responsibilities can include the administration of methadone, counselling and health education, and client care coordination with other agencies on behalf of the client. CAMH's interprofessional *Opioid Dependence Treatment Certificate Program* is also recommended for nurses.

To recruit nurses, you can:
· get a list of local nurses from a nursing association or nurse contact
· invite nurses to an information session
· enlist a subject-matter expert to facilitate the meeting
· invite other appropriate supporters to make presentations at the meeting, such as other nurses or doctors who work with methadone clients, clients and members of the working group
· show the documentary *Prescription for Addiction* (DVD)
· present clinical research and support materials about MMT, its benefits, your project plan and training opportunities
· supply attendees with contact information for the working group and CAMH where they can get more information
· ask physicians involved in the program to help recruit nurses.

Health and Social Support Services

You should strive to include health and social support services in your program and establish partnerships with them. Which services you are able to include will depend on the services available in your community and your resources to engage additional services. Services you may wish to consider for your program include:
· general counselling
· primary health care
· mental health care
· social assistance
· financial assistance
· child care assistance
· supportive housing
· employment assistance.

Reconnect with the people you met during the earlier planning stages from local addiction treatment and mental agencies, public health units, social service departments and other related agencies. Members of the working group may be representatives from these agencies or have close ties to them. These working group members can create links and help establish successful partnerships to ensure that support services are included in the program.

"Partnerships are key. They spread the load and lend credibility to your project."

—MMT case manager

While many of these potential partners may be interested in participating in the program, they may not have the staff or funding available to provide the necessary counselling and case management services. (See below.)

Secure resources and funding

During the development phase, you will also need to determine your operating costs and secure resources and funding for the program. Working groups often have to be creative and collaborative to make an MMT program work with little or no funding. Partnerships with other agencies and community support services offer several cost-saving options. You will need to establish whether these options offer one-time or ongoing support for your projected operating costs.

"If you can gain the acceptance of your local government, getting a letter of support may improve your chances of receiving funding."

—CAMH program consultant

Agencies and community support services that you partner with can:
· provide services at their location
· share some of their staff members to fill your personnel requirements
· offer space and infrastructure on their premises
· pool their funding with yours to hire new staff or pay for other operating costs.

To apply for additional funding to operate your MMT program, you can submit your action plan and program model to your LHIN and/or the Ministry of Health and Long-Term Care.

"When applying for funding, be specific about how your treatment program will reduce the impact on hospitals, especially at emergency departments. Develop an evaluation plan up front and include it in your application."

—MMT program director

Determine the service delivery model

Generally, MMT programs involve a multidisciplinary network of service providers, often operating out of several different locations. MMT services may be delivered in a variety of different settings, including:
· substance use treatment services or clinics (outpatient/inpatient)
· community health centres or clinics
· family health teams
· private medical clinics
· multidisciplinary group practice
· individual physicians' offices and community pharmacies
· hospital-based health clinics
· HIV/AIDS services or clinics
· mental health agencies
· correctional facilities.

Having defined your program's goals, identified client and provider needs, established partnerships and determined your resources, the service delivery model of your program will begin to take shape. While you may ideally favour a clinic model with all services operating out of one site, your physicians may prefer to operate out of their own practice. Or you may not have the financial resources to open a new clinic. Research has not yet proven one model to be superior over another (Health Canada, 2002a).

Shape a service delivery model that works best for your clients, service providers and community. Your model should strive to provide:
· easy access to services for clients
· a model that promotes treatment retention
· effective and efficient service procedures and communication among providers
· value to the community.

Choose the setting that suits your model and community resources. The best setting for your program is the one you can afford and that matches the needs of the clients, the community, the service providers and partners.

You should:
- ensure the site(s) has the necessary infrastructure for service delivery
- choose a setting with easy access (close to public transportation and parking)
- consult with the community.

A SAFE AND COMFORTABLE PLACE

Consider the physical appearance and infrastructure of the site where clients will be receiving treatment. Create an environment they will want to visit—where they feel safe and supported.
- Keep the inside of the treatment centre or office well-maintained.
- Improve and maintain the physical environment outside the treatment centre or office.
- Give clients a place to congregate to foster peer support.
- Minimize wait times.
- Maintain flow of clients into and out of the clinic that is respectful of clients, their time and the community.
- Consider the needs of those bringing children with them—make the space child friendly.

Draft a logic model

A logic model is a description of the goals of your program and the resources you will use to achieve your results. Logic models are often presented as a chart or diagram. For your program, a logic model helps present and share your understanding of the relationships among the resources you have to operate your program, the services you plan to offer and the impact or results you hope to achieve.

In its simplest form, the logic model can be organized into five steps:
- inputs: resources available to do the work, such as money, service providers, staff and equipment
- activities: work that the program does with the resources or inputs
- outputs: immediate results of the activities, service delivered to clients

· outcomes: long-term results of delivering outputs
· impact: change resulting from the outputs and outcomes that have affected the community as a whole.

By using a logic model to describe your program, you can easily define your work and measure it. Performance measures and analysis can be drawn from any of the five steps (W.K. Kellogg Foundation, 2004).

"It's important not to look at methadone as the only solution to opioid dependence.... It's important that people have a wide range of choices in terms of how they manage their illness, and that people have access to different choices at different stages of their treatment."
—family physician and MMT prescriber

Implementing the program

Before the MMT program can receive clients, the working group, along with the physicians and other key service providers, should map the transition from development to implementation. The systematic preparation and consultation work that you did in the previous stages will help you to implement the program.

Develop an implementation plan

An implementation plan will assist you in moving the project from development to service provision. Implementation plans will vary from community to community. Use your implementation plan to:
· determine a time line for implementation
· train and educate service providers
· define roles and responsibilities of service providers
· develop written protocols for referrals
· develop communication protocols among service providers and the working group
· develop policies and procedures (See *Policies and procedures* on page 73.)
· confirm performance indicators based on your logic model.

Before receiving clients, ensure that all members of the MMT program team (the service providers and working group):
· have received MMT-specific training and education
· agree to and understand the policies, protocols and procedures of the program
· are prepared and equipped to take on clients.

"Talking about starting a methadone clinic is one thing...actual bricks and mortar are another thing altogether. Continue to involve the community in this process and stay proactive rather than reactive in this phase."

—CAMH program consultant

Time lines, roles and responsibilities

Determine essential milestones and establish a clear time line to ensure that all members of the team are ready to receive clients when the program opens. Some physicians and other service providers may only want to take on a limited number of clients when the program first opens. In this case, establish expected time lines and a review of the services to decide how and when the program will be fully operational and able to meet capacity.

Clearly define the roles and responsibilities of the service providers, partner agencies, clients, the working group and the community advisory committee (if applicable). Sharing these descriptions with the entire team will help build a cohesive program in which team members respect and recognize the contributions of their colleagues.

Training for service providers

All MMT service providers should receive MMT-specific training and education before the program starts. The *Opiate Dependence Treatment Interprofessional Education Program* offered by CAMH is required for physicians and pharmacists and recommended for nurses and counsellors. Physicians are also required to get special exemption under the federal *Controlled Drugs and Substances Act* to be able to prescribe methadone.

The CAMH education program prepares MMT health care professionals to provide a comprehensive range of services for people who are dependent on opioids. These services include assessment for opioid dependence, methadone or buprenorphine maintenance treatments when appropriate, counselling, case management and referral to withdrawal management services, if appropriate.

You can help plan and organize local education opportunities for service providers. For example, experienced MMT physicians and other service providers can give workshops, presentations and consultation support specifically tailored to the team and service delivery model of the program. Education workshops should also include informing team members of the policies, procedures and protocols of the program. (See below.)

Additionally, all service providers should be aware of other available education resources, such as:
· *Best Practices: Methadone Maintenance Treatment* (Health Canada) 2002
· *Methadone Maintenance Guidelines* (CPSO) 2005
· *Methadone Maintenance Treatment: Best Practices in Case Management* (CAMH) 2009 (in press)
· *Methadone Maintenance: A Counsellor's Guide to Treatment* (CAMH) 2003
· *Methadone Maintenance: A Pharmacist's Guide to Treatment,* 2nd Edition (CAMH) 2004
· *Methadone Maintenance: A Physician's Guide to Treatment,* 2nd Edition (CAMH) 2008.
· *Methadone Maintenance Treatment: Client Handbook* (CAMH) 2008.

For a full listing, see *Resources* on page 93.

Policies and procedures

Developing written policies and procedures can help avoid potential problems when service begins. A program policy manual provides a set of guidelines to help the team manage the day-to-day care of clients.

> Kingston's Street Health Centre—a harm reduction health centre—developed a comprehensive policy manual for its methadone treatment clinic in 2004 and revised it in 2008. It includes information about the centre's program design, policies and procedures, eligibility criteria, MMT client agreement and medical directives. Street Health Centre's *Policy Manual* provides an excellent template that you can adapt to reflect your own program and client base. For a copy of the manual, contact the Street Health Centre at info@streethealth.kchc.ca.

◁ TIP

Referral protocols

Successful implementation relies on clearly defined systems of referral, especially when the services are not provided at one site. Outline a protocol to assist in the referral of clients to the MMT program. Make sure everyone (i.e., MMT providers, clients and partners) are aware of the referral process to avoid any unnecessary delays or confusion.

Communication protocols

A well-articulated communication protocol among the program team members and between the service providers and the working group is equally important as a strong system of referral. The communication protocol should outline the need for ongoing communication between team members, while respecting the need for client confidentiality.

A reliable communication link between the team and the working group helps address any problems or areas that need attention in a timely manner. It also provides an avenue to discuss opportunities to enhance service delivery.

Procedures

Certain elements of your service delivery model may require establishing a procedure to ensure consistency among service providers and to help manage the needs and expectations of clients. For example, in its 2008 revised *Policy Manual,* the Street Health Centre outlined procedures for:
· methadone overdose
· recording missed methadone doses
· dispensing fentanyl patches
· detention centre transfers
· pharmacy transfers.

For your implementation plan, draft those procedures for which you anticipate a need. Once the program is running, you can review and revise your draft procedures and create new ones where appropriate.

Policies

Clear program policies are associated with longer retention in treatment and improved treatment outcomes. The policies you develop should be tailored to meet the needs of your program model, client base and health care provider needs. Develop policies that promote ease of access to a client-centred model of care. Health Canada's *Best Practices: Methadone Maintenance Treatment* (2002a) identified the following treatment policy areas as key:

· open admission
· timely assessment
· adequate, individualized dosage
· methadone dosage during pregnancy
· unlimited duration of treatment
· clear discharge criteria
· non-punitive approach to drug use during treatment
· client-centred management of tapering.

The Street Health Centre (2008) established policies in the following areas for their MMT program:

· use of opioid medications
· use of benzodiazepines
· vomited doses of methadone
· missed doses of methadone
· missed appointments
· carry privileges
· urine toxicology and collection protocol
· client conduct/onsite violence
· criminal activity at the centre
· confidentiality
· cash payment for methadone
· duplicate names.

Whatever policies you choose to develop, it is important that program rules are clearly outlined and that they are applied consistently. To help ensure client understanding and agreement with the policies, develop a client–provider treatment and confidentiality agreement. This agreement should outline the conditions under which clients are typically admitted to treatment, the rules they are generally required to adhere to and what they can expect. Review the agreement, the program's policies and expectations as well as the mandatory informed consent with the client. Be sure to give them the opportunity to ask questions prior to signing the agreement and before starting treatment.

TIP ▷

CAMH provides a sample client–provider agreement in their online resources for professionals. The sample agreement was created by Dr. Michael Lester and Dr. Lisa Lefebvre, CAMH. You can adapt it to reflect your own specific circumstances. The document is part of the *Clinic Toolkit for Methadone and Buprenorphine Providers* available at http://methadonesaveslives.ca.

Recruit clients

Your implementation plan should also include client recruitment. Given the stigma and marginalization people who are dependent on opioids often experience, client outreach is a necessary and ongoing part of operation.

Consider proactive recruitment of potential clients who are not likely to access treatment without encouragement and support. You can recruit clients by:
· using peer-based strategies and networks
· partnering with agencies working at the front line or "street" level
· providing information and increasing awareness of your program to health care and social service agencies, physicians, addiction assessment referral centres, addiction and mental health treatment providers.

TIP ▷

Make sure clients know what they can expect and that they have options. MMT is not for everyone. They need to know that, even if they have tried MMT in the past, they can try MMT again or seek other forms of treatment. They should know that their relapse may have been linked to the particular program, rather than to their personal failure.

Redefine the role of the working group

The role of the community working group needs to be reviewed by the program team once the program has been implemented. During implementation and early stages of the new program, the working group's supportive role will be vital to the program team. Over time, the working group's role will likely evolve to a program advisory capacity.

The purpose and responsibilities of the working group post-implementation should be determined and approved by the group's members and the program's service providers. When defining the role of the working group, include a clear description of its duties and the time commitment required of the members.

Many working groups continue to provide support to the program and the service providers once the program is in operation. The working group can:
· examine and help resolve problem issues
· address unmet client needs
· assist with ongoing client outreach
· support ongoing recruitment of additional service providers
· set up training and education workshops
· facilitate networking with partners and potential new partners
· establish and liaise with community advisory group (local residents)
· participate in ongoing community engagement
· monitor and evaluate the program.

"Anticipate change. What looks great on paper may need some tweaking once you go live."

—MMT program director

Evaluating
the program

Evaluation is an ongoing process that can help refine and improve the quality of the program's service delivery. Through evaluation, the program team can measure how well the program is meeting its objectives and the needs of clients.

Develop an evaluation plan

Develop an evaluation plan that will ensure continuous improvement of the quality of the program's services and their delivery. In the plan, outline the tools and indicators that will be used for evaluation and detail how often the program will be evaluated. Use your logic model to help develop your evaluation plan.

The plan should:
· review the goals of the program
· determine the indicators for evaluation of the program
· identify the barriers to and determinants of positive outcomes
· monitor the program's impact on clients and the community
· measure the program's cost-effectiveness
· identify how the evaluation results will be disseminated and to whom.

The types of evaluation you may consider for your plan include (Street Health Centre, 2008):
· needs assessment
· evaluation assessment
· procedure evaluation

· cost analysis
· satisfaction evaluation (i.e., of clients, service providers and
  the community)
· outcome evaluation
· economic evaluation.

> *"Evaluation is crucial. Funding bodies will require that you continually monitor and evaluate your progress."*
>
> —MMT *program director*

Program goals

Clients, service providers, the community and the working group may have different, albeit inter-related, goals for the program. Consequently, everyone's definition of success may be different. Furthermore, the goals of the program may also change as the program matures.

Your program evaluation should include a review of the goals that were established for the program. (See *Define goals and identify resources and barriers* on page 55.) Assess whether the goals are still applicable or should be revised based on the findings of the evaluation.

> *"Addiction needs to be looked at with less morality and more reality."*
>
> —*street-wise harm reduction worker*

Evaluation indicators

Choose specific indicators and tools to measure the evaluation of treatment outcomes. Align your outcome indicators with your LHIN's indicators. These will include measurements that show the program's impact on the health care system, such as reduced number of hospitalizations and use of emergency departments.

The Street Health Centre (2008) includes the following indicators in their evaluation:
· client retention: length of stay in treatment and treatment termination
· program compliance: adherence to program guidelines
· utilization of services: number and nature of services (e.g., medical, psychosocial, social support and referral)

- addiction recovery: incidence of drug use, extent of polysubstance and problem drug use
- general health and well-being: general assessment of function, measurement of health status and psychiatric co-morbidity.

Program impact

Your program's impact can be measured through client and community satisfaction surveys and through various satisfaction measures (Street Health Centre, 2008), such as:
- treatment activities
- comprehensiveness of treatment
- continuity of treatment
- staff performance
- treatment environment.

Satisfaction surveys
General-use satisfaction surveys can be modified and used to measure satisfaction among clients and community members. Results of these surveys provide important feedback for evaluation, such as:
- the extent to which the program's services are meeting client and community expectations
- information that can lead to improvements to service delivery.

Participation in surveys must be voluntary and conducted in a manner that protects the identity and confidentiality of participants.

Suggestion box
A physical (suggestion box) and electronic (website) anonymous feedback mechanism can be used for gathering useful information from clients, the community and program team members.

Service provider feedback
You can also conduct interviews or develop questionnaires to gather feedback from the program's service providers. They can give you their opinions about the impact of the program on clients, the effectiveness of the program's policies and procedures, where they see need for improvement and whether their needs are being met.

"Evaluating and improving upon your services will lead to the best quality of care for the individuals you serve."

—*MMT program director*

Identify the role of the working group in evaluation

The working group, along with the assistance and approval of the service providers, may be involved in the development of an evaluation plan and evaluation tools. The working group can help:
· develop an evaluation plan and tools
· define new program elements identified by evaluation
· recruit additional service providers
· hire administrative staff
· implement feedback mechanisms in the community.

Appendix:
Do You Know...
Methadone

This appendix is taken from *Do You Know... Methadone* (CAMH) 2003, one in a series of drug information brochures. Reprinted with permission.

What is it?

Street Names: juice, meth (also used to refer to methamphetamines)

Methadone belongs to the opioid family of drugs. It is used most commonly to treat dependence on other opioid drugs, such as heroin, codeine and morphine.

Methadone is a "synthetic" opioid, which means that it is made from chemicals in a lab. Other opioid drugs include the "opiates," such as morphine and codeine, which are natural products of the opium poppy, and "semi-synthetic" opioids, such as heroin, which is morphine that has been chemically processed.

Methadone was developed in Germany during the Second World War and was first used to provide pain relief.

Methadone maintenance treatment, which prevents opioid withdrawal and reduces or eliminates drug cravings, was first developed in the 1960s. For many years, Canadian regulations around the prescription of methadone were so restrictive that few doctors offered the treatment. People who wanted methadone treatment often had to wait months or years. In the 1990s, the need to reduce the harm of drug use was more clearly recognized, and changes were made to make it easier for doctors to provide methadone treatment. This has led to an increase in the number of people receiving treatment, and a decrease in the number of heroin-related deaths.

Methadone maintenance is not a "cure": it is a treatment. Through treatment, people who are dependent on opioids receive the medical and social support they need to stabilize and improve their lives. They are encouraged to stay in treatment for as long as it helps them.

What does methadone look like?

Pure methadone is a white crystalline powder. The powder is dissolved, usually in a fruit-flavoured drink, and is taken orally once a day.

Who uses methadone?

Most people who are prescribed methadone are being treated for dependence on opioid drugs. This includes people who are dependent on illicit opioids, such as heroin, and also prescription opioids, such as codeine.

Women who use opioid drugs regularly and who are pregnant are often treated with methadone to protect the fetus. Short-acting opioids such as heroin must be taken frequently to avoid withdrawal. Opioid withdrawal increases the risk of miscarriage or premature birth. Methadone maintenance, combined with medical care, improves the chances of having a healthy baby. There are no known long-term effects of methadone on the baby.

People who use opioid drugs regularly, and who are infected with HIV or hepatitis C, are prescribed methadone treatment to help protect their health, and to reduce the risk of spreading infection through needle sharing.

Methadone is sometimes used to provide pain relief for people who have severe chronic pain or pain associated with terminal illness.

How does methadone make you feel?

When people begin methadone treatment, some experience the euphoria and sedation that are common to all opioid drugs. As treatment continues, and a stable dose of methadone is established, tolerance to these effects develops. Those in treatment often describe the feeling of being on methadone as "normal." Methadone treatment does not interfere with their thinking. They can work, go to school or care for family. Methadone also blocks the euphoric effect of heroin and other opioids, and in this way reduces the use of these drugs.

Most people experience some side-effects from methadone treatment. Possible side-effects include sweating, constipation and weight gain.

How long does the effect last?

A person who is opioid-dependent is kept free of withdrawal symptoms for 24 hours with a single dose of methadone. In contrast, a person who uses heroin to avoid withdrawal must use three to four times a day.

Daily treatment with methadone may continue indefinitely. If, however, the person taking methadone and his or her doctor agree to move toward ending treatment, the methadone dose is tapered down gradually over many weeks or months, easing the process of withdrawal.

If methadone is stopped abruptly, symptoms such as stomach cramps, diarrhea and muscle and bone ache will occur. These symptoms begin within one to three days after the last dose, peak at three to five days, and then gradually subside, although other symptoms such as sleep problems and drug cravings may continue for months.

Is methadone dangerous?

When methadone is taken as prescribed, it is very safe and will not cause any damage to internal organs or thinking, even when taken daily for many years. On the other hand, methadone is a powerful drug and can be extremely dangerous to people who do not take it regularly, as they have no tolerance for its effects. Even a small amount may be fatal for a child. For this reason, the dispensing of methadone is carefully monitored and controlled.

An important benefit of methadone treatment is that it reduces heroin use. The dangers of heroin use include death by overdose, and becoming infected, through needle sharing, with viruses such as HIV and hepatitis C. Methadone treatment helps to protect people from heroin-related tragedies.

Is methadone addictive?

Modern definitions of "addiction" look at many factors in assessing a person's drug use. These include "tolerance," or the need to use increasing amounts to achieve the same effect; "physical dependence," resulting in withdrawal symptoms if drug use is stopped; and "compulsive use," despite the negative consequences of continuing to use the drug.

Some people say that methadone is just as "addictive" as heroin. People in methadone treatment do become tolerant to certain effects of the drug, and will experience withdrawal if they do not take their regular dose. But methadone fails to meet a full definition of "addictive" when we look at how and why the drug is used.

First of all, methadone maintenance is offered as a medical treatment, and is prescribed only to people who are already dependent on opioid drugs. For these people, methadone provides a safe alternative to the routine danger and desperation of securing a steady supply of street drugs such as heroin. It frees them from the nagging compulsion to use, and allows them a chance to focus on improving their lives.

Methadone is sometimes used as a street drug, but when it is, it is usually taken to prevent symptoms of heroin withdrawal. The effects of methadone come on too slowly and last too long to give it much appeal as a substance of abuse.

What are the long-term effects of methadone?

Methadone maintenance is a long-term treatment. Length of treatment varies, from a year or two to 20 years or more. This prolonged treatment with proper doses of methadone is medically safe and is the most effective treatment currently available for opioid dependence.

References

Bell, J. & Zador, D. (2000). A risk-benefit analysis of methadone maintenance treatment. *Drug Safety, 22* (3), 179–90.

Brands, B., Blake, J., Sproule, B., Gourlay, D. & Busto, U. (2004). Prescription opioid abuse in patients presenting for methadone maintenance treatment. *Drug and Alcohol Dependence, 73* (2), 199–207.

Callaly, T., Trauer, T., Munro, L. & Whelan, G. (2001). Prevalence of psychiatric disorder in a methadone maintenance population. *Australian and New Zealand Journal of Psychiatry, 35* (5), 601–5.

Centre for Addiction and Mental Health. (2008). *Methadone Maintenance Treatment: Client Handbook.* Available:
http://www.camh.net/Care_Treatment/Resources_clients_families_friends/
Methadone_Maintenance_Treatment/mmt_client_hndbk.pdf. Retrieved January 2009.

Collège des médecins du Québec and Ordre des pharmaciens du Québec. (2008). *The Use of Buprenorphine in the Treatment of Opiate Addiction.* Available:
http://www.cmq.org/en/public/profil/commun/AProposOrdre/~/media/351D36F81
0B94FDDABFF70022BA76B47.ashx?sc_lang=en. Retrieved March 2009.

College of Physicians and Surgeons of Ontario. (2009a). *Buprenorphine Hydrochloride for the Treatment of Opioid Dependence.* Available:
http://www.cpso.on.ca/policies/policies/default.aspx?ID=1826. Retrieved March 2009.

College of Physicians and Surgeons of Ontario. (2009b). *Fact Sheet for Methadone Program.* Available:
https://www.cpso.on.ca/uploadedFiles/MethadoneFactSheet(1).pdf. Retrieved February 2009.

College of Physicians and Surgeons of Ontario. (2005). *Methadone Maintenance Guidelines.* Available:
http://www.cpso.on.ca/uploadedFiles/policies/guidelines/methadone/
Meth%20Guidelines%20_Oct07.pdf. Retrieved January 2009.

Fischer, B., Cape, D., Daniel, N. & Gliksman, L. (2002). Methadone treatment in Ontario after the 1996 regulation reforms: Results of a physician survey. *Annales de Médecine Interne, 153* (7 Suppl), 2S11–21.

References

Fischer, B. & Rehm, J. (1997). The case for a heroin substitution treatment trial in Canada. *Canadian Journal of Public Health, 88* (6), 367–70.

Fischer, B., Rehm, J., Patra, J. & Cruz, M.F. (2006). Changes in illicit opioid use across Canada. *Canadian Medical Association Journal, 175* (11), 1385.

Gossop, M., Stewart, D., Browne, N. & Marsden, J. (2003). Methadone treatment for opiate dependent patients in general practice and specialist clinic settings: Outcomes at 2-year follow-up. *Journal of Substance Abuse Treatment, 24* (4), 313–21.

Hart, W. (2007). *Report of the Methadone Maintenance Treatment Practices Task Force.* Ontario Ministry of Health and Long-Term Care. Available: http://www.health.gov.on.ca/english/public/pub/ministry_reports/methadone_taskforce/methadone_taskforce.pdf. Retrieved January 2009.

Health Canada: Office of Canada's Drug Strategy. (2002a). *Best Practices: Methadone Maintenance Treatment.* Available: http://www.hc-sc.gc.ca/hl-vs/alt_formats/hecs-sesc/pdf/pubs/adp-apd/methadone/litreview_methadone_maint_treat.pdf. Retrieved January 2009.

Health Canada: Office of Canada's Drug Strategy. (2002b). *Literature Review: Methadone Maintenance Treatment.* Available: http://www.hc-sc.gc.ca/hl-vs/alt_formats/hecs-sesc/pdf/pubs/adp-apd/methadone/litreview_methadone_maint_treat.pdf. Retrieved January 2009.

Health Canada: Office of Canada's Drug Strategy. (2002c). *Methadone Maintenance Treatment.* Available: http://www.hc-sc.gc.ca/hl-vs/alt_formats/hecs-sesc/pdf/pubs/adp-apd/methadone-treatment-traitement/methadone-treatment-traitement_e.pdf. Retrieved January 2009.

W.K. Kellogg Foundation. (2004). *Logic Model Development Guide.* Available: http://www.wkkf.org/Pubs/Tools/Evaluation/Pub3669.pdf. Retrieved March 2009.

NIH Consensus Conference. (1998). Effective medical treatment of opiate addiction. National Consensus Development Panel on Effective Medical Treatment of Opiate Addiction. *Journal of the American Medical Association, 280* (22),1936–43.

Pang, L., Hao, Y., Mi, G., Wang, C., Luo, W., Rou, K. et al. (2007). Effectiveness of first eight methadone maintenance treatment clinics in China. *AIDS, 21* (8 Suppl), S103–7.

Sproule, B., Brands, B., Li, S. & Catz-Biro, L. (2009). Changing patterns in opioid addiction: Characterizing users of oxycodone and other opioids. *Canadian Family Physician, 55* (1), 68–9.

Street Health Centre. (2008). *Methadone Treatment Clinic Policy Manual.* Kingston: Kingston Community Health Centre.

Strike, C.J., Urbanoski, K., Fischer, B., Marsh, D.C. & Millson, M. (2005). Policy changes and the methadone maintenance treatment system for opioid dependence in Ontario, 1996 to 2001. *Journal of Addictive Diseases, 24* (1), 39–51.

Wilson, K., MacIntosh, J. & Getty, G. (2007). 'Tapping a tie': Successful partnerships in managing addictions with methadone. *Issues in Mental Health Nursing, 28* (9), 977–96.

World Health Organization: Office on Drugs and Crime. (2004). *WHO/UNODC/UNAIDS Position Paper: Substitution Maintenance Therapy in the Management of Opioid Dependence and HIV/AIDS Prevention.* Available: http://www.unodc.org/docs/treatment/Brochure_E.pdf. Retrieved January 2009.

Also consulted

[No authors listed]. (1998). Consensus panel proposes sweeping changes to improve access to methadone maintenance treatment. *American Society of Health-System Pharmacists, 55* (3), 208, 210.

Birnbaum, H.G., White, A.G., Reynolds, J.L., Greenberg, P.E., Zhang, M., Vallow, S. et al. (2006). Estimated costs of prescription opioid analgesic abuse in the United States in 2001: A societal perspective. *The Clinical Journal of Pain, 22* (8), 667–76.

Centre for Addiction and Mental Health. (2003). *Do You Know... Methadone.* Available: http://www.camh.net/Care_Treatment/Resources_clients_families_friends/Methadone_Maintenance_Treatment/index.html. Retrieved January 2009.

Centre for Addiction and Mental Health. (2003). *Do You Know... Opioids.* Available: http://www.camh.net/Care_Treatment/Resources_clients_families_friends/Methadone_Maintenance_Treatment/index.html. Retrieved January 2009.

Millson, P.E., Challacombe, L., Villeneuve, P.J., Fischer, B., Strike, C.J., Myers, T. et al. (2004). Self-perceived health among Canadian opiate users: A comparison to the general population and to other chronic disease populations. *Canadian Journal of Public Health, 95* (2), 99–103.

Popova, S., Rehm, J. & Fischer, B. (2006). An overview of illegal opioid use and health services utilization in Canada. *Public Health, 120* (4), 320–8.

Sheridan, J., Goodyear-Smith, F., Butler, R., Wheeler, A. & Gohns, A. (2008). Barriers to, and incentives for, the transfer of opioid-dependent people on methadone maintenance treatment from secondary care to primary health care. *Drug and Alcohol Review, 27* (2), 178–84.

Sheridan, J., Manning, V., Ridge, G., Mayet, S. & Strang, J. (2007). Community pharmacies and the provision of opioid substitution services for drug misusers: Changes in activity and attitudes of community pharmacists across England 1995–2005. *Addiction, 102* (11), 1824–30.

Wodak, A. (2002). Methadone and heroin prescription: Babies and bath water. *Substance Use & Misuse, 37* (4), 523–31.

Resources

This listing of resources offers a selection of materials about MMT *. The Canadian and Ontario experience is highlighted. Resources mentioned within the guide are included in this listing.

Publications

* To order any CAMH publication, contact Sales and Distribution, Centre for Addiction and Mental Health toll-free 1-800-661-1111, in Toronto 416-595-6059 or e-mail publications@camh.net. For more details about each publication, see the CAMH Publications Catalogue available at www.camh.net/Publications.

Brands, Bruna (editor), Meldon Kahan, Peter Selby & Lynn Wilson (associate editors). (2000). *Management of Alcohol, Tobacco and Other Drug Problems: A Physician's Manual.* Toronto: Centre for Addiction and Mental Health.

Kahan, Meldon & Lynn Wilson (editors). (2002). *Managing Alcohol, Tobacco and Other Drug Problems: A Pocket Guide for Physicians and Nurses.* Toronto: Centre for Addiction and Mental Health.

Kahan, Meldon & Peter Selby (editors). (2008). *Methadone Maintenance: A Physician's Guide to Treatment* (2nd ed.). Toronto: Centre for Addiction and Mental Health.

Martin, Garth, Bruna Brands & David C. Marsh (editors). (2003). *Methadone Maintenance: A Counsellor's Guide to Treatment.* Toronto: Centre for Addiction and Mental Health.

Isaac, Pearl, Anne Kalvick, John Brands & Eva Janecek (editors). (2004). *Methadone Maintenance: A Pharmacist's Guide to Treatment* (2nd ed.). Toronto: Centre for Addiction and Mental Health.

Tschakovsky, Kate (author) & Lynn Schellenberg (editor). (2009). *Methadone Maintenance Treatment: Best Practices in Case Management.* Toronto: Centre for Addiction and Mental Health. In press.

Centre for Addiction and Mental Health. (2008). *Methadone Maintenance Treatment: Selected Bibliography.* Toronto: Centre for Addiction and Mental Health. Available: http://www.camh.net/About_Addiction_Mental_Health/CAMH_Library/methadone2008.pdf.

College of Physicians and Surgeons of Ontario. (2005). *Methadone Maintenance Guidelines.* Toronto: College of Physicians and Surgeons of Ontario. Available: http://www.cpso.on.ca/uploadedFiles/policies/guidelines/methadone/Meth%20Guidelines%20_Oct07.pdf.

Office of Canada's Drug Strategy. (2002). *Best Practices Methadone Maintenance Treatment.* Ottawa: Health Canada. Available: http://www.hc-sc.gc.ca/hl-vs/alt_formats/hecs-sesc/pdf/pubs/adp-apd/methadone-bp-mp/methadone-bp-mp-eng.pdf.

Hart, W. Anton. (2007). *Report of the Methadone Maintenance Treatment Practices Task Force.* Toronto: Ontario Ministry of Health and Long-Term Care. Available: http://www.health.gov.on.ca/english/public/pub/ministry_reports/methadone_taskforce/methadone_taskforce.pdf.

Centre for Addiction and Mental Health. (2008). *Methadone Maintenance Treatment: Client Handbook.* Toronto: Centre for Addiction and Mental Health. Available: http://www.camh.net/Care_Treatment/Resources_clients_families_friends/Methadone_Maintenance_Treatment/index.html.

Centre for Addiction and Mental Health. (2002). *Methadone Maintenance Treatment: Information for Clients* [Web page and brochure]. Toronto: Centre for Addiction and Mental Health. Available: http://www.camh.net/About_Addiction_Mental_Health/Drug_and_Addiction_Information/methadone_therapy.html.

Centre for Addiction and Mental Health *Methadone Saves Lives* series of MMT brochures:
· Addiction Counsellors and Methadone Maintenance Treatment
· Health Care Professionals and Methadone Maintenance Treatment
· Prescription Painkillers and Methadone Maintenance Treatment

Methadone Saves Lives brochures available:
http://www.camh.net/care_treatment/program_descriptions/opiate/opiate_professionals.html.

Centre for Addiction and Mental Health *Do You Know...* series of drug information brochures:
· Alcohol
· Alcohol, Other Drugs and Driving
· Amphetamines
· Benzodiazepines
· Caffeine
· Cannabis
· Cocaine
· Ecstasy
· GHB
· Hallucinogens
· Heroin
· Inhalants
· Ketamine
· LSD
· Methadone
· Methamphetamine
· Opioids
· Rohypnol
· Steroids
· Tobacco

Centre for Addiction and Mental Health *Straight Talk* series of harm reduction drug information brochures:

- Crack
- OxyContin
- Methamphetamine
- Street Methadone

Do You Know... and *Straight Talk* brochures available:
www.camh.net/About_Addiction_Mental_Health/Drug_and_Addiction_Information/index.html.

Toolkits

Methadone Saves Lives

http://methadonesaveslives.ca
MethadoneSavesLives.ca provides professionals and people living with opioid drug problems with the information they need to make informed decisions about MMT.

Clinic Toolkit for
Methadone and Buprenorphine Providers

This toolkit provides forms, letter templates and quick references for practitioners involved in methadone and/or buprenorphine maintenance treatment in outpatient settings in Ontario.
http://www.camh.net/Publications/Resources_for_Professionals/clinic_toolkit_methadone/clinic_toolkit_methadone.html

Prescription for Addiction Kit

The kit includes a DVD (short version) of the compelling documentary *Prescription for Addiction* that examines the growing problem of dependence and addiction to opioid pain medications; a comprehensive User Guide offering support for facilitators, teachers and others wishing to screen the film in their communities; and a promotional flyer. The DVD and guide was produced by Sky Works Charitable Foundation and commissioned by CAMH in partnership with the Ontario Federation of Community Mental Health and Addiction Programs and St. Joseph's Health Care Group, Thunder Bay.
http://www.camh.net/Care_Treatment/Program_Descriptions/opiate/Prescription_for_Addiction_Kit.html

Training

Opiate Dependence Treatment Interprofessional Education
Program (CAMH)

This program prepares physicians, pharmacists, nurses and counsellors to provide a comprehensive range of services for people with opioid dependence, including assessment for opioid dependence, methadone or buprenorphine maintenance treatments when appropriate, counselling, case management, and referral to withdrawal management services if appropriate.
Note: This program replaces the Methadone Maintenance Treatment (MMT) Workshop and Online Course
http://www.camh.net/education/Classroom_courses_forums_events/opiate_interprof_treat_course.html

CAMH: Relevant services

Addiction Clinical Consultation Service

Tel: 416 595-6968 or toll free 1 888 720-2227
Hours of operation: 8:00 a.m. to 4:00 p.m., Monday to Friday.
CAMH provides health care professionals with an MMT caseload with access to educational resources. Staff will assess your query and the appropriate consultant will return your call.
http://www.camh.net/About_CAMH/Guide_to_CAMH/Mental_Health_Programs/
General_Psychiatry_Program/Addiction_Clinical_Consultation_Service

CAMH Provincial Services Offices

CAMH provides health promotion, prevention services and training across the province.
http://www.camh.net/About_CAMH/Ontario_Regional_Services/index.html

CAMH's main offices are located in Toronto with a system of 10 local offices throughout Ontario, along with a number of staff working from home office locations. Staff are distributed across six provincial areas that fall within the Policy, Education and Health Promotion (PEHP) Division: Southwestern, West Central, GTA West, Central, Eastern and Northern Ontario Areas.

Hamilton
20 Hughson Street South, Suite 804
Hamilton, ON L8N 2A1
Tel: 905 525-1250
Fax: 905 527-6957

Kenora
301 First Avenue South, 2nd Floor
Banister Centre
Kenora, ON P9N 1W2
Tel: 807 468-6372
Fax: 807 468-5257

Kingston
27 Place d'Armes, Suite 200
Kingston, ON K7K 6Z6
Tel: 613 546-4266
Fax: 613 546-3931

London
100 Collip Circle, Suite 200
London, ON N6G 4X8
Tel: 519 858-5110
Fax: 519 858-5133

North Bay
60 Champlain Street, Suite 101
North Bay, ON P1B 7M4
Tel: 705 472-3850
Fax: 705 472-8397

Ottawa
150 Isabella Street
Suite 205, Phase 1
Ottawa, ON K1S 1V7
Tel: 613 569-6024
Fax: 613 569-6117

Sault Ste. Marie
421 Bay Street, Suite 302
Sault Ste. Marie, ON P6A 1X3
Tel: 705 256-2226
Fax: 705 256-8233

Sudbury
888 Regent Street, Suite 302
Sudbury, ON P3E 6C6
Tel: 705 675-1195
Fax: 705 675-9121

Thunder Bay
200 Syndicate Avenue South, Suite 401
Thunder Bay, ON P3E 1C9
Tel: 807 626-8111
Fax: 807 626-9090

Windsor
3200 Deziel Drive, Suite 118
Windsor, ON N8W 5K8
Tel: 519 251-0500
Fax: 519 251-0494

CAMH McLaughlin Information Centre

This information centre provides a toll-free information line, including information and referral specialists, telephone support line staffed by volunteers providing informal and/or peer support, on-line information and print materials.
219 Dufferin Street (at King), Suite 3B
Toronto, ON
Tel: 416 595-6111 or toll free 1 800 463-6273
mclaughlininformation@camh.net

Other organizations

The College of Physicians and Surgeons of Ontario
80 College Street
Toronto, ON M5G 2E2
Tel: 416 967-2661 or toll free 1 800 268-7096 ext. 661
www.cpso.on.ca

The mandate of the College of Physicians and Surgeons methadone program since its inception in June of 1996 has been to improve the quality and accessibility of MMT in Ontario.

In 1996, following the reduction of involvement by the Federal Bureau of Drug Surveillance, the College entered into a formal partnership with the Ministry of Health's Ontario Substance Abuse Bureau through a funding agreement. The CPSO entered into a close working relationship with the Ontario College of Pharmacists and the Centre for Addiction and Mental Health. This partnership has enhanced the availability of methadone maintenance treatment in Ontario through the outreach activities of the partners and the recruitment of individual physicians and pharmacists to make methadone available for the treatment of opiate dependence.

Program activities
Centralized registry of all exempted physicians
The Physician Registry captures the practice information of each physician issued an exemption by Health Canada including their name, address, telephone number. Additionally, the type (analgesia or opioid) of exemption and effective dates of the exemption are tracked for each physician who prescribes methadone under the *Controlled Drugs and Substances Act, 1996*.

Assessments for physicians with an exemption to prescribe methadone
Assessments for physicians with an exemption to prescribe methadone for opioid dependence are part of an ongoing quality assurance program at CPSO. The program assesses each physician who holds an exemption to prescribe methadone. For new physicians entering the program, the assessment is conducted during their first year of practice and is intended to evaluate physician compliance with the MMT guidelines using an 18 point checklist and to provide feedback and educational support to the prescribing physician.

Centralized patient registry for methadone maintenance treatment
The registry captures basic information such as name, date of birth, gender for each patient registered to a physician in a methadone program for the treatment of opioid dependence.

Patient/Physician requests for entry into treatment or transfer between prescribers
The methadone program receives patient treatment forms from physicians for initiations, cessations and transfers of patients wishing to enter or who are already on a methadone program. Prescribers register and de-register their patients with the program in order to reduce the danger of double doctoring, which could harm or potentially kill patients and expose the community to illicit methadone trafficking.

Program staff receives a significant number of telephone inquiries on a wide range of issues, which include, for example, identifying local methadone prescribers in the patients' area, assisting the doctor's office in locating a pharmacy or transferring a patient to another location, assisting physicians who are seeking guidance regarding their methadone practices and responding to pharmacy inquiries about exempted prescribers.

Recruitment of physicians to prescribe methadone for opioid dependence
The program continues to participate in outreach, education and recruitment activities across the province. The program will try to work with any community that expresses an interest in additional information. Currently the program is working with the Ontario College of Family Physicians on a pilot recruitment initiative for family physicians who want to work in this area.

Guidelines for methadone maintenance treatment
In 2001, the College of Physicians and Surgeons of Ontario, the Ontario College of Pharmacists and the Centre for Addiction and Mental Health, in consultation with physicians experienced in providing methadone treatment, developed MMT guidelines that were updated in 2005 and provide the framework for physicians who practice in this area. The College wants to keep the profession up to date with information on current best practices and standards in this area of medicine and therefore undertakes to update the MMT guidelines regularly. The College will be publishing updated MMT guidelines in 2010.

Registered Nurses' Association of Ontario
158 Pearl Street
Toronto, ON M5H 1L3
Tel: 416 599-1925 or toll free 1 800 268-7199
www.rnao.org

The Registered Nurses' Association of Ontario (RNAO) is the professional association representing registered nurses in Ontario. It is the strong, credible voice leading the nursing profession to influence and promote healthy public policy.

RNAO Best Practice Guideline—Supporting Clients on Methadone Maintenance Treatment (MMT)

The established goal of the guideline is to provide nurses with recommendations, based on the best available evidence, related to nursing knowledge and support for clients who are either a potential candidate for or already on methadone maintenance treatment for opiate dependence. It is intended for nurses who are not necessarily experts in this area of practice, who work in a variety of practice settings, across the continuum of care.

E-learning education series on addictions

The addictions e-learning series considers adult learning principles and is a self-directed program that is available online supporting holistic care provided to support clients on methadone maintenance treatment. Some modules include, but are not limited to, principles of addictions, harm reduction, health promotion, client-centred care, therapeutic relationships and crisis intervention.

Ontario College of Pharmacists
483 Huron Street
Toronto, ON M5R 2R4
Tel: 416 962-4861 ext. 236
www.ocpinfo.com

The Ontario College of Pharmacists (OCP) is the registering and regulating body for pharmacy practice in Ontario. All pharmacists in Ontario who compound medications and dispense prescriptions to the public must first have met the professional qualifications set by the college, and be registered as a pharmacist. Likewise, all pharmacies must meet certain standards for operations and be accredited by the college. In addition to setting initial standards, the college ensures ongoing adherence to the professional and operational standards. Pharmacists who dispense methadone must be aware of the policies and guidelines for methadone set out by OCP.

Methadone Maintenance Treatment (MMT): Interim policy information

On March 15, 2006, Health Canada advised OCP of its support for the new *Ontario College of Pharmacists Interim Policy for the Provision of Methadone in Ontario*. The interim policy was developed in collaboration with CPSO and in consultation with Health Canada with the view to permit an MMT model in Ontario that meets the needs of MMT patients. For more information, visit:
http://www.ocpinfo.com/client/ocp/OCPHome.nsf/d12550e436a1716585256ac90065aa1c/c824df4c0ede6983852573e50055d157?OpenDocument&Highlight=2,Methadone

ConnexOntario—Drug and Alcohol Registry of Treatment
Tel: 519 439-0174 or toll free 1 800 565-8603
http://www.connexontario.ca/index.html

ConnexOntario Health Services Information is a corporation whose mandate is to improve access to alcohol and drug, gambling and mental health services for the people of Ontario. ConnexOntario operates the Drug and Alcohol Registry of Treatment (DART), the Ontario Problem Gambling Helpline (OPGH) and Mental Health Service Information Ontario (MHSIO), which provide information and referral to services in Ontario.

www.ingramcontent.com/pod-product-compliance
Lightning Source LLC
Chambersburg PA
CBHW081658270326
41933CB00017B/3214